Bash Reference Manual

Reference Documentation for Bash
Edition 4.4, for **Bash** Version 4.4.
September 2016

Chet Ramey, Case Western Reserve University
Brian Fox, Free Software Foundation

This text is a brief description of the features that are present in the Bash shell (version 4.4, 7 September 2016).

This is Edition 4.4, last updated 7 September 2016, of *The GNU Bash Reference Manual*, for `Bash`, Version 4.4.

Table of Contents

1 Introduction

1.1 What is Bash?

Bash is the shell, or command language interpreter, for the GNU operating system. The name is an acronym for the 'Bourne-Again SHell', a pun on Stephen Bourne, the author of the direct ancestor of the current Unix shell `sh`, which appeared in the Seventh Edition Bell Labs Research version of Unix.

Bash is largely compatible with `sh` and incorporates useful features from the Korn shell `ksh` and the C shell `csh`. It is intended to be a conformant implementation of the IEEE POSIX Shell and Tools portion of the IEEE POSIX specification (IEEE Standard 1003.1). It offers functional improvements over `sh` for both interactive and programming use.

While the GNU operating system provides other shells, including a version of `csh`, Bash is the default shell. Like other GNU software, Bash is quite portable. It currently runs on nearly every version of Unix and a few other operating systems − independently-supported ports exist for MS-DOS, OS/2, and Windows platforms.

1.2 What is a shell?

At its base, a shell is simply a macro processor that executes commands. The term macro processor means functionality where text and symbols are expanded to create larger expressions.

A Unix shell is both a command interpreter and a programming language. As a command interpreter, the shell provides the user interface to the rich set of GNU utilities. The programming language features allow these utilities to be combined. Files containing commands can be created, and become commands themselves. These new commands have the same status as system commands in directories such as `/bin`, allowing users or groups to establish custom environments to automate their common tasks.

Shells may be used interactively or non-interactively. In interactive mode, they accept input typed from the keyboard. When executing non-interactively, shells execute commands read from a file.

A shell allows execution of GNU commands, both synchronously and asynchronously. The shell waits for synchronous commands to complete before accepting more input; asynchronous commands continue to execute in parallel with the shell while it reads and executes additional commands. The *redirection* constructs permit fine-grained control of the input and output of those commands. Moreover, the shell allows control over the contents of commands' environments.

Shells also provide a small set of built-in commands (*builtins*) implementing functionality impossible or inconvenient to obtain via separate utilities. For example, `cd`, `break`, `continue`, and `exec` cannot be implemented outside of the shell because they directly manipulate the shell itself. The `history`, `getopts`, `kill`, or `pwd` builtins, among others, could be implemented in separate utilities, but they are more convenient to use as builtin commands. All of the shell builtins are described in subsequent sections.

While executing commands is essential, most of the power (and complexity) of shells is due to their embedded programming languages. Like any high-level language, the shell provides variables, flow control constructs, quoting, and functions.

Shells offer features geared specifically for interactive use rather than to augment the programming language. These interactive features include job control, command line editing, command history and aliases. Each of these features is described in this manual.

2 Definitions

These definitions are used throughout the remainder of this manual.

POSIX   A family of open system standards based on Unix. Bash is primarily concerned with the Shell and Utilities portion of the POSIX 1003.1 standard.

blank   A space or tab character.

builtin   A command that is implemented internally by the shell itself, rather than by an executable program somewhere in the file system.

control operator

A **token** that performs a control function. It is a **newline** or one of the following: '||', '&&', '&', ';', ';;', ';&', ';;&', '|', '|&', '(', or ')'.

exit status

The value returned by a command to its caller. The value is restricted to eight bits, so the maximum value is 255.

field   A unit of text that is the result of one of the shell expansions. After expansion, when executing a command, the resulting fields are used as the command name and arguments.

filename   A string of characters used to identify a file.

job   A set of processes comprising a pipeline, and any processes descended from it, that are all in the same process group.

job control

A mechanism by which users can selectively stop (suspend) and restart (resume) execution of processes.

metacharacter

A character that, when unquoted, separates words. A metacharacter is a **space**, **tab**, **newline**, or one of the following characters: '|', '&', ';', '(', ')', '<', or '>'.

name   A **word** consisting solely of letters, numbers, and underscores, and beginning with a letter or underscore. **Names** are used as shell variable and function names. Also referred to as an **identifier**.

operator   A **control operator** or a **redirection operator**. See Section 3.6 [Redirections], page 32, for a list of redirection operators. Operators contain at least one unquoted **metacharacter**.

process group

A collection of related processes each having the same process group ID.

process group ID

A unique identifier that represents a **process group** during its lifetime.

reserved word

A **word** that has a special meaning to the shell. Most reserved words introduce shell flow control constructs, such as **for** and **while**.

return status
A synonym for **exit status**.

signal   A mechanism by which a process may be notified by the kernel of an event occurring in the system.

special builtin
A shell builtin command that has been classified as special by the POSIX standard.

token   A sequence of characters considered a single unit by the shell. It is either a **word** or an **operator**.

word   A sequence of characters treated as a unit by the shell. Words may not include unquoted **metacharacters**.

3 Basic Shell Features

Bash is an acronym for 'Bourne-Again SHell'. The Bourne shell is the traditional Unix shell originally written by Stephen Bourne. All of the Bourne shell builtin commands are available in Bash, The rules for evaluation and quoting are taken from the POSIX specification for the 'standard' Unix shell.

This chapter briefly summarizes the shell's 'building blocks': commands, control structures, shell functions, shell *parameters*, shell expansions, *redirections*, which are a way to direct input and output from and to named files, and how the shell executes commands.

3.1 Shell Syntax

When the shell reads input, it proceeds through a sequence of operations. If the input indicates the beginning of a comment, the shell ignores the comment symbol ('#'), and the rest of that line.

Otherwise, roughly speaking, the shell reads its input and divides the input into words and operators, employing the quoting rules to select which meanings to assign various words and characters.

The shell then parses these tokens into commands and other constructs, removes the special meaning of certain words or characters, expands others, redirects input and output as needed, executes the specified command, waits for the command's exit status, and makes that exit status available for further inspection or processing.

3.1.1 Shell Operation

The following is a brief description of the shell's operation when it reads and executes a command. Basically, the shell does the following:

1. Reads its input from a file (see Section 3.8 [Shell Scripts], page 40), from a string supplied as an argument to the -c invocation option (see Section 6.1 [Invoking Bash], page 82), or from the user's terminal.

2. Breaks the input into words and operators, obeying the quoting rules described in Section 3.1.2 [Quoting], page 6. These tokens are separated by metacharacters. Alias expansion is performed by this step (see Section 6.6 [Aliases], page 90).

3. Parses the tokens into simple and compound commands (see Section 3.2 [Shell Commands], page 8).

4. Performs the various shell expansions (see Section 3.5 [Shell Expansions], page 21), breaking the expanded tokens into lists of filenames (see Section 3.5.8 [Filename Expansion], page 30) and commands and arguments.

5. Performs any necessary redirections (see Section 3.6 [Redirections], page 32) and removes the redirection operators and their operands from the argument list.

6. Executes the command (see Section 3.7 [Executing Commands], page 36).

7. Optionally waits for the command to complete and collects its exit status (see Section 3.7.5 [Exit Status], page 39).

3.1.2 Quoting

Quoting is used to remove the special meaning of certain characters or words to the shell. Quoting can be used to disable special treatment for special characters, to prevent reserved words from being recognized as such, and to prevent parameter expansion.

Each of the shell metacharacters (see Chapter 2 [Definitions], page 3) has special meaning to the shell and must be quoted if it is to represent itself. When the command history expansion facilities are being used (see Section 9.3 [History Interaction], page 139), the *history expansion* character, usually '!', must be quoted to prevent history expansion. See Section 9.1 [Bash History Facilities], page 137, for more details concerning history expansion.

There are three quoting mechanisms: the *escape character*, single quotes, and double quotes.

3.1.2.1 Escape Character

A non-quoted backslash '\' is the Bash escape character. It preserves the literal value of the next character that follows, with the exception of `newline`. If a `\newline` pair appears, and the backslash itself is not quoted, the `\newline` is treated as a line continuation (that is, it is removed from the input stream and effectively ignored).

3.1.2.2 Single Quotes

Enclosing characters in single quotes ('') preserves the literal value of each character within the quotes. A single quote may not occur between single quotes, even when preceded by a backslash.

3.1.2.3 Double Quotes

Enclosing characters in double quotes ("") preserves the literal value of all characters within the quotes, with the exception of '$', '`', '\', and, when history expansion is enabled, '!'. When the shell is in POSIX mode (see Section 6.11 [Bash POSIX Mode], page 96), the '!' has no special meaning within double quotes, even when history expansion is enabled. The characters '$' and '`' retain their special meaning within double quotes (see Section 3.5 [Shell Expansions], page 21). The backslash retains its special meaning only when followed by one of the following characters: '$', '`', '"', '\', or `newline`. Within double quotes, backslashes that are followed by one of these characters are removed. Backslashes preceding characters without a special meaning are left unmodified. A double quote may be quoted within double quotes by preceding it with a backslash. If enabled, history expansion will be performed unless an '!' appearing in double quotes is escaped using a backslash. The backslash preceding the '!' is not removed.

The special parameters '*' and '@' have special meaning when in double quotes (see Section 3.5.3 [Shell Parameter Expansion], page 23).

3.1.2.4 ANSI-C Quoting

Words of the form `$'string'` are treated specially. The word expands to *string*, with backslash-escaped characters replaced as specified by the ANSI C standard. Backslash escape sequences, if present, are decoded as follows:

`\a`   alert (bell)

`\b`   backspace

`\e`	
`\E`	an escape character (not ANSI C)
`\f`	form feed
`\n`	newline
`\r`	carriage return
`\t`	horizontal tab
`\v`	vertical tab
`\\`	backslash
`\'`	single quote
`\"`	double quote
`\?`	question mark
`\nnn`	the eight-bit character whose value is the octal value *nnn* (one to three digits)
`\xHH`	the eight-bit character whose value is the hexadecimal value *HH* (one or two hex digits)
`\uHHHH`	the Unicode (ISO/IEC 10646) character whose value is the hexadecimal value *HHHH* (one to four hex digits)
`\UHHHHHHHH`	the Unicode (ISO/IEC 10646) character whose value is the hexadecimal value *HHHHHHHH* (one to eight hex digits)
`\cx`	a control-*x* character

The expanded result is single-quoted, as if the dollar sign had not been present.

3.1.2.5 Locale-Specific Translation

A double-quoted string preceded by a dollar sign ('`$`') will cause the string to be translated according to the current locale. If the current locale is `C` or `POSIX`, the dollar sign is ignored. If the string is translated and replaced, the replacement is double-quoted.

Some systems use the message catalog selected by the `LC_MESSAGES` shell variable. Others create the name of the message catalog from the value of the `TEXTDOMAIN` shell variable, possibly adding a suffix of '`.mo`'. If you use the `TEXTDOMAIN` variable, you may need to set the `TEXTDOMAINDIR` variable to the location of the message catalog files. Still others use both variables in this fashion: `TEXTDOMAINDIR`/`LC_MESSAGES`/`LC_MESSAGES`/`TEXTDOMAIN`.mo.

3.1.3 Comments

In a non-interactive shell, or an interactive shell in which the `interactive_comments` option to the `shopt` builtin is enabled (see Section 4.3.2 [The Shopt Builtin], page 64), a word beginning with '`#`' causes that word and all remaining characters on that line to be ignored. An interactive shell without the `interactive_comments` option enabled does not allow comments. The `interactive_comments` option is on by default in interactive shells. See Section 6.3 [Interactive Shells], page 85, for a description of what makes a shell interactive.

3.2 Shell Commands

A simple shell command such as `echo a b c` consists of the command itself followed by arguments, separated by spaces.

More complex shell commands are composed of simple commands arranged together in a variety of ways: in a pipeline in which the output of one command becomes the input of a second, in a loop or conditional construct, or in some other grouping.

3.2.1 Simple Commands

A simple command is the kind of command encountered most often. It's just a sequence of words separated by `blanks`, terminated by one of the shell's control operators (see Chapter 2 [Definitions], page 3). The first word generally specifies a command to be executed, with the rest of the words being that command's arguments.

The return status (see Section 3.7.5 [Exit Status], page 39) of a simple command is its exit status as provided by the POSIX 1003.1 `waitpid` function, or 128+n if the command was terminated by signal n.

3.2.2 Pipelines

A `pipeline` is a sequence of one or more commands separated by one of the control operators '`|`' or '`|&`'.

The format for a pipeline is

```
[time [-p]] [!] command1 [ | or |& command2 ] ...
```

The output of each command in the pipeline is connected via a pipe to the input of the next command. That is, each command reads the previous command's output. This connection is performed before any redirections specified by the command.

If '`|&`' is used, *command1*'s standard error, in addition to its standard output, is connected to *command2*'s standard input through the pipe; it is shorthand for `2>&1 |`. This implicit redirection of the standard error to the standard output is performed after any redirections specified by the command.

The reserved word `time` causes timing statistics to be printed for the pipeline once it finishes. The statistics currently consist of elapsed (wall-clock) time and user and system time consumed by the command's execution. The `-p` option changes the output format to that specified by POSIX. When the shell is in POSIX mode (see Section 6.11 [Bash POSIX Mode], page 96), it does not recognize `time` as a reserved word if the next token begins with a '`-`'. The `TIMEFORMAT` variable may be set to a format string that specifies how the timing information should be displayed. See Section 5.2 [Bash Variables], page 71, for a description of the available formats. The use of `time` as a reserved word permits the timing of shell builtins, shell functions, and pipelines. An external `time` command cannot time these easily.

When the shell is in POSIX mode (see Section 6.11 [Bash POSIX Mode], page 96), `time` may be followed by a newline. In this case, the shell displays the total user and system time consumed by the shell and its children. The `TIMEFORMAT` variable may be used to specify the format of the time information.

If the pipeline is not executed asynchronously (see Section 3.2.3 [Lists], page 9), the shell waits for all commands in the pipeline to complete.

Each command in a pipeline is executed in its own subshell (see Section 3.7.3 [Command Execution Environment], page 37). The exit status of a pipeline is the exit status of the last command in the pipeline, unless the `pipefail` option is enabled (see Section 4.3.1 [The Set Builtin], page 60). If `pipefail` is enabled, the pipeline's return status is the value of the last (rightmost) command to exit with a non-zero status, or zero if all commands exit successfully. If the reserved word '!' precedes the pipeline, the exit status is the logical negation of the exit status as described above. The shell waits for all commands in the pipeline to terminate before returning a value.

3.2.3 Lists of Commands

A `list` is a sequence of one or more pipelines separated by one of the operators ';', '&', '&&', or '||', and optionally terminated by one of ';', '&', or a `newline`.

Of these list operators, '&&' and '||' have equal precedence, followed by ';' and '&', which have equal precedence.

A sequence of one or more newlines may appear in a `list` to delimit commands, equivalent to a semicolon.

If a command is terminated by the control operator '&', the shell executes the command asynchronously in a subshell. This is known as executing the command in the *background*. The shell does not wait for the command to finish, and the return status is 0 (true). When job control is not active (see Chapter 7 [Job Control], page 100), the standard input for asynchronous commands, in the absence of any explicit redirections, is redirected from `/dev/null`.

Commands separated by a ';' are executed sequentially; the shell waits for each command to terminate in turn. The return status is the exit status of the last command executed.

AND and OR lists are sequences of one or more pipelines separated by the control operators '&&' and '||', respectively. AND and OR lists are executed with left associativity.

An AND list has the form

    command1 && command2

command2 is executed if, and only if, *command1* returns an exit status of zero.

An OR list has the form

    command1 || command2

command2 is executed if, and only if, *command1* returns a non-zero exit status.

The return status of AND and OR lists is the exit status of the last command executed in the list.

3.2.4 Compound Commands

Compound commands are the shell programming constructs. Each construct begins with a reserved word or control operator and is terminated by a corresponding reserved word or operator. Any redirections (see Section 3.6 [Redirections], page 32) associated with a compound command apply to all commands within that compound command unless explicitly overridden.

In most cases a list of commands in a compound command's description may be separated from the rest of the command by one or more newlines, and may be followed by a newline in place of a semicolon.

Bash provides looping constructs, conditional commands, and mechanisms to group commands and execute them as a unit.

3.2.4.1 Looping Constructs

Bash supports the following looping constructs.

Note that wherever a ';' appears in the description of a command's syntax, it may be replaced with one or more newlines.

until
> The syntax of the `until` command is:
>
>   until test-commands; do consequent-commands; done
>
> Execute *consequent-commands* as long as *test-commands* has an exit status which is not zero. The return status is the exit status of the last command executed in *consequent-commands*, or zero if none was executed.

while
> The syntax of the `while` command is:
>
>   while test-commands; do consequent-commands; done
>
> Execute *consequent-commands* as long as *test-commands* has an exit status of zero. The return status is the exit status of the last command executed in *consequent-commands*, or zero if none was executed.

for
> The syntax of the `for` command is:
>
>   for name [[in [words ...]] ;] do commands; done
>
> Expand *words*, and execute *commands* once for each member in the resultant list, with *name* bound to the current member. If 'in *words*' is not present, the `for` command executes the *commands* once for each positional parameter that is set, as if 'in "$@"' had been specified (see Section 3.4.2 [Special Parameters], page 20). The return status is the exit status of the last command that executes. If there are no items in the expansion of *words*, no commands are executed, and the return status is zero.
>
> An alternate form of the `for` command is also supported:
>
>   for ((expr1 ; expr2 ; expr3)) ; do commands ; done
>
> First, the arithmetic expression *expr1* is evaluated according to the rules described below (see Section 6.5 [Shell Arithmetic], page 89). The arithmetic expression *expr2* is then evaluated repeatedly until it evaluates to zero. Each time *expr2* evaluates to a non-zero value, *commands* are executed and the arithmetic expression *expr3* is evaluated. If any expression is omitted, it behaves as if it evaluates to 1. The return value is the exit status of the last command in *commands* that is executed, or false if any of the expressions is invalid.

The `break` and `continue` builtins (see Section 4.1 [Bourne Shell Builtins], page 42) may be used to control loop execution.

3.2.4.2 Conditional Constructs

if
> The syntax of the `if` command is:
>
>   if test-commands; then
>   consequent-commands;

```
[elif more-test-commands; then
  more-consequents;]
[else alternate-consequents;]
fi
```

The *test-commands* list is executed, and if its return status is zero, the *consequent-commands* list is executed. If *test-commands* returns a non-zero status, each `elif` list is executed in turn, and if its exit status is zero, the corresponding *more-consequents* is executed and the command completes. If 'else *alternate-consequents*' is present, and the final command in the final `if` or `elif` clause has a non-zero exit status, then *alternate-consequents* is executed. The return status is the exit status of the last command executed, or zero if no condition tested true.

case   The syntax of the `case` command is:

```
case word in [ [(] pattern [| pattern]...) command-list ;;]... esac
```

`case` will selectively execute the *command-list* corresponding to the first *pattern* that matches *word*. If the `nocasematch` shell option (see the description of `shopt` in Section 4.3.2 [The Shopt Builtin], page 64) is enabled, the match is performed without regard to the case of alphabetic characters. The '|' is used to separate multiple patterns, and the ')' operator terminates a pattern list. A list of patterns and an associated command-list is known as a *clause*.

Each clause must be terminated with ';;', ';&', or ';;&'. The *word* undergoes tilde expansion, parameter expansion, command substitution, arithmetic expansion, and quote removal before matching is attempted. Each *pattern* undergoes tilde expansion, parameter expansion, command substitution, and arithmetic expansion.

There may be an arbitrary number of `case` clauses, each terminated by a ';;', ';&', or ';;&'. The first pattern that matches determines the command-list that is executed. It's a common idiom to use '*' as the final pattern to define the default case, since that pattern will always match.

Here is an example using `case` in a script that could be used to describe one interesting feature of an animal:

```
echo -n "Enter the name of an animal: "
read ANIMAL
echo -n "The $ANIMAL has "
case $ANIMAL in
  horse | dog | cat) echo -n "four";;
  man | kangaroo ) echo -n "two";;
  *) echo -n "an unknown number of";;
esac
echo " legs."
```

If the ';;' operator is used, no subsequent matches are attempted after the first pattern match. Using ';&' in place of ';;' causes execution to continue with the *command-list* associated with the next clause, if any. Using ';;&' in place of ';;' causes the shell to test the patterns in the next clause, if any, and execute any associated *command-list* on a successful match.

The return status is zero if no *pattern* is matched. Otherwise, the return status is the exit status of the *command-list* executed.

select

The `select` construct allows the easy generation of menus. It has almost the same syntax as the `for` command:

    select *name* [in *words* ...]; do *commands*; done

The list of words following `in` is expanded, generating a list of items. The set of expanded words is printed on the standard error output stream, each preceded by a number. If the '`in words`' is omitted, the positional parameters are printed, as if '`in "$@"`' had been specified. The `PS3` prompt is then displayed and a line is read from the standard input. If the line consists of a number corresponding to one of the displayed words, then the value of *name* is set to that word. If the line is empty, the words and prompt are displayed again. If `EOF` is read, the `select` command completes. Any other value read causes *name* to be set to null. The line read is saved in the variable `REPLY`.

The *commands* are executed after each selection until a `break` command is executed, at which point the `select` command completes.

Here is an example that allows the user to pick a filename from the current directory, and displays the name and index of the file selected.

    select fname in *;
    do
    echo you picked $fname \($REPLY\)
    break;
    done

((...))

    ((*expression*))

The arithmetic *expression* is evaluated according to the rules described below (see Section 6.5 [Shell Arithmetic], page 89). If the value of the expression is non-zero, the return status is 0; otherwise the return status is 1. This is exactly equivalent to

    let "*expression*"

See Section 4.2 [Bash Builtins], page 49, for a full description of the `let` builtin.

[[...]]

    [[*expression*]]

Return a status of 0 or 1 depending on the evaluation of the conditional expression *expression*. Expressions are composed of the primaries described below in Section 6.4 [Bash Conditional Expressions], page 87. Word splitting and filename expansion are not performed on the words between the [[and]]; tilde expansion, parameter and variable expansion, arithmetic expansion, command substitution, process substitution, and quote removal are performed. Conditional operators such as '`-f`' must be unquoted to be recognized as primaries.

When used with [[, the '<' and '>' operators sort lexicographically using the current locale.

When the '==' and '!=' operators are used, the string to the right of the operator is considered a pattern and matched according to the rules described below in Section 3.5.8.1 [Pattern Matching], page 31, as if the `extglob` shell option were enabled. The '=' operator is identical to '=='. If the `nocasematch` shell option (see the description of `shopt` in Section 4.3.2 [The Shopt Builtin], page 64) is enabled, the match is performed without regard to the case of alphabetic characters. The return value is 0 if the string matches ('==') or does not match ('!=')the pattern, and 1 otherwise. Any part of the pattern may be quoted to force the quoted portion to be matched as a string.

An additional binary operator, '=~', is available, with the same precedence as '==' and '!='. When it is used, the string to the right of the operator is considered an extended regular expression and matched accordingly (as in *regex3*)). The return value is 0 if the string matches the pattern, and 1 otherwise. If the regular expression is syntactically incorrect, the conditional expression's return value is 2. If the `nocasematch` shell option (see the description of `shopt` in Section 4.3.2 [The Shopt Builtin], page 64) is enabled, the match is performed without regard to the case of alphabetic characters. Any part of the pattern may be quoted to force the quoted portion to be matched as a string. Bracket expressions in regular expressions must be treated carefully, since normal quoting characters lose their meanings between brackets. If the pattern is stored in a shell variable, quoting the variable expansion forces the entire pattern to be matched as a string. Substrings matched by parenthesized subexpressions within the regular expression are saved in the array variable `BASH_REMATCH`. The element of `BASH_REMATCH` with index 0 is the portion of the string matching the entire regular expression. The element of `BASH_REMATCH` with index n is the portion of the string matching the nth parenthesized subexpression.

For example, the following will match a line (stored in the shell variable *line*) if there is a sequence of characters in the value consisting of any number, including zero, of space characters, zero or one instances of 'a', then a 'b':

```
[[ $line =~ [[:space:]]*(a)?b ]]
```

That means values like 'aab' and ' aaaaaab' will match, as will a line containing a 'b' anywhere in its value.

Storing the regular expression in a shell variable is often a useful way to avoid problems with quoting characters that are special to the shell. It is sometimes difficult to specify a regular expression literally without using quotes, or to keep track of the quoting used by regular expressions while paying attention to the shell's quote removal. Using a shell variable to store the pattern decreases these problems. For example, the following is equivalent to the above:

```
pattern='[[:space:]]*(a)?b'
[[ $line =~ $pattern ]]
```

If you want to match a character that's special to the regular expression grammar, it has to be quoted to remove its special meaning. This means that in the pattern 'xxx.txt', the '.' matches any character in the string (its usual regular expression meaning), but in the pattern '"xxx.txt"' it can only match a literal '.'. Shell programmers should take special care with backslashes, since backslashes are used both by the shell and regular expressions to remove the special meaning from the following character. The following two sets of commands are *not* equivalent:

```
pattern='\.'

[[ . =~ $pattern ]]
[[ . =~ \. ]]

[[ . =~ "$pattern" ]]
[[ . =~ '\.' ]]
```

The first two matches will succeed, but the second two will not, because in the second two the backslash will be part of the pattern to be matched. In the first two examples, the backslash removes the special meaning from '.', so the literal '.' matches. If the string in the first examples were anything other than '.', say 'a', the pattern would not match, because the quoted '.' in the pattern loses its special meaning of matching any single character.

Expressions may be combined using the following operators, listed in decreasing order of precedence:

(*expression*)
> Returns the value of *expression*. This may be used to override the normal precedence of operators.

! *expression*
> True if *expression* is false.

expression1* && *expression2
> True if both *expression1* and *expression2* are true.

expression1* || *expression2
> True if either *expression1* or *expression2* is true.

The **&&** and **||** operators do not evaluate *expression2* if the value of *expression1* is sufficient to determine the return value of the entire conditional expression.

3.2.4.3 Grouping Commands

Bash provides two ways to group a list of commands to be executed as a unit. When commands are grouped, redirections may be applied to the entire command list. For example, the output of all the commands in the list may be redirected to a single stream.

()

> **(*list*)**
>
> Placing a list of commands between parentheses causes a subshell environment to be created (see Section 3.7.3 [Command Execution Environment], page 37), and each of the commands in *list* to be executed in that subshell. Since the *list* is executed in a subshell, variable assignments do not remain in effect after the subshell completes.

{}

> **{ *list*; }**

Placing a list of commands between curly braces causes the list to be executed in the current shell context. No subshell is created. The semicolon (or newline) following *list* is required.

In addition to the creation of a subshell, there is a subtle difference between these two constructs due to historical reasons. The braces are **reserved words**, so they must be separated from the *list* by **blanks** or other shell metacharacters. The parentheses are **operators**, and are recognized as separate tokens by the shell even if they are not separated from the *list* by whitespace.

The exit status of both of these constructs is the exit status of *list*.

3.2.5 Coprocesses

A `coprocess` is a shell command preceded by the `coproc` reserved word. A coprocess is executed asynchronously in a subshell, as if the command had been terminated with the '&' control operator, with a two-way pipe established between the executing shell and the coprocess.

The format for a coprocess is:

```
coproc [NAME] command [redirections]
```

This creates a coprocess named *NAME*. If *NAME* is not supplied, the default name is *COPROC*. *NAME* must not be supplied if *command* is a simple command (see Section 3.2.1 [Simple Commands], page 8); otherwise, it is interpreted as the first word of the simple command.

When the coprocess is executed, the shell creates an array variable (see Section 6.7 [Arrays], page 91) named NAME in the context of the executing shell. The standard output of *command* is connected via a pipe to a file descriptor in the executing shell, and that file descriptor is assigned to NAME[0]. The standard input of *command* is connected via a pipe to a file descriptor in the executing shell, and that file descriptor is assigned to NAME[1]. This pipe is established before any redirections specified by the command (see Section 3.6 [Redirections], page 32). The file descriptors can be utilized as arguments to shell commands and redirections using standard word expansions. The file descriptors are not available in subshells.

The process ID of the shell spawned to execute the coprocess is available as the value of the variable NAME_PID. The `wait` builtin command may be used to wait for the coprocess to terminate.

Since the coprocess is created as an asynchronous command, the `coproc` command always returns success. The return status of a coprocess is the exit status of *command*.

3.2.6 GNU Parallel

There are ways to run commands in parallel that are not built into Bash. GNU Parallel is a tool to do just that.

GNU Parallel, as its name suggests, can be used to build and run commands in parallel. You may run the same command with different arguments, whether they are filenames, usernames, hostnames, or lines read from files. GNU Parallel provides shorthand references to many of the most common operations (input lines, various portions of the input line, different ways to specify the input source, and so on). Parallel can replace `xargs` or feed commands from its input sources to several different instances of Bash.

For a complete description, refer to the GNU Parallel documentation. A few examples should provide a brief introduction to its use.

For example, it is easy to replace `xargs` to gzip all html files in the current directory and its subdirectories:

```
find . -type f -name '*.html' -print | parallel gzip
```

If you need to protect special characters such as newlines in file names, use find's `-print0` option and parallel's `-0` option.

You can use Parallel to move files from the current directory when the number of files is too large to process with one `mv` invocation:

```
ls | parallel mv {} destdir
```

As you can see, the {} is replaced with each line read from standard input. While using `ls` will work in most instances, it is not sufficient to deal with all filenames. If you need to accommodate special characters in filenames, you can use

```
find . -depth 1 \! -name '.*' -print0 | parallel -0 mv {} destdir
```

as alluded to above.

This will run as many `mv` commands as there are files in the current directory. You can emulate a parallel `xargs` by adding the `-X` option:

```
find . -depth 1 \! -name '.*' -print0 | parallel -0 -X mv {} destdir
```

GNU Parallel can replace certain common idioms that operate on lines read from a file (in this case, filenames listed one per line):

```
while IFS= read -r x; do
do-something1 "$x" "config-$x"
do-something2 < "$x"
done < file | process-output
```

with a more compact syntax reminiscent of lambdas:

```
cat list | parallel "do-something1 {} config-{} ; do-something2 < {}" | process-outp
```

Parallel provides a built-in mechanism to remove filename extensions, which lends itself to batch file transformations or renaming:

```
ls *.gz | parallel -j+0 "zcat {} | bzip2 >{.}.bz2 && rm {}"
```

This will recompress all files in the current directory with names ending in .gz using bzip2, running one job per CPU (-j+0) in parallel. (We use `ls` for brevity here; using `find` as above is more robust in the face of filenames containing unexpected characters.) Parallel can take arguments from the command line; the above can also be written as

```
parallel "zcat {} | bzip2 >{.}.bz2 && rm {}" ::: *.gz
```

If a command generates output, you may want to preserve the input order in the output. For instance, the following command

```
{ echo foss.org.my ; echo debian.org; echo freenetproject.org; } | parallel tracerou
```

will display as output the traceroute invocation that finishes first. Adding the `-k` option

```
{ echo foss.org.my ; echo debian.org; echo freenetproject.org; } | parallel -k trace
```

will ensure that the output of `traceroute foss.org.my` is displayed first.

Finally, Parallel can be used to run a sequence of shell commands in parallel, similar to 'cat file | bash'. It is not uncommon to take a list of filenames, create a series of shell commands to operate on them, and feed that list of commnds to a shell. Parallel can speed this up. Assuming that `file` contains a list of shell commands, one per line,

```
parallel -j 10 < file
```

will evaluate the commands using the shell (since no explicit command is supplied as an argument), in blocks of ten shell jobs at a time.

3.3 Shell Functions

Shell functions are a way to group commands for later execution using a single name for the group. They are executed just like a "regular" command. When the name of a shell function is used as a simple command name, the list of commands associated with that function name is executed. Shell functions are executed in the current shell context; no new process is created to interpret them.

Functions are declared using this syntax:

```
name () compound-command [ redirections ]
```

or

```
function name [()] compound-command [ redirections ]
```

This defines a shell function named *name*. The reserved word `function` is optional. If the `function` reserved word is supplied, the parentheses are optional. The *body* of the function is the compound command *compound-command* (see Section 3.2.4 [Compound Commands], page 9). That command is usually a *list* enclosed between { and }, but may be any compound command listed above, with one exception: If the `function` reserved word is used, but the parentheses are not supplied, the braces are required. *compound-command* is executed whenever *name* is specified as the name of a command. When the shell is in POSIX mode (see Section 6.11 [Bash POSIX Mode], page 96), *name* may not be the same as one of the special builtins (see Section 4.4 [Special Builtins], page 70). Any redirections (see Section 3.6 [Redirections], page 32) associated with the shell function are performed when the function is executed.

A function definition may be deleted using the `-f` option to the `unset` builtin (see Section 4.1 [Bourne Shell Builtins], page 42).

The exit status of a function definition is zero unless a syntax error occurs or a readonly function with the same name already exists. When executed, the exit status of a function is the exit status of the last command executed in the body.

Note that for historical reasons, in the most common usage the curly braces that surround the body of the function must be separated from the body by `blanks` or newlines. This is because the braces are reserved words and are only recognized as such when they are separated from the command list by whitespace or another shell metacharacter. Also, when using the braces, the *list* must be terminated by a semicolon, a '&', or a newline.

When a function is executed, the arguments to the function become the positional parameters during its execution (see Section 3.4.1 [Positional Parameters], page 19). The special parameter '#' that expands to the number of positional parameters is updated to reflect the change. Special parameter 0 is unchanged. The first element of the `FUNCNAME` variable is set to the name of the function while the function is executing.

All other aspects of the shell execution environment are identical between a function and its caller with these exceptions: the `DEBUG` and `RETURN` traps are not inherited unless the function has been given the `trace` attribute using the `declare` builtin or the `-o functrace` option has been enabled with the `set` builtin, (in which case all functions inherit the DEBUG and RETURN traps), and the ERR trap is not inherited unless the `-o errtrace` shell option has been enabled. See Section 4.1 [Bourne Shell Builtins], page 42, for the description of the `trap` builtin.

The FUNCNEST variable, if set to a numeric value greater than 0, defines a maximum function nesting level. Function invocations that exceed the limit cause the entire command to abort.

If the builtin command `return` is executed in a function, the function completes and execution resumes with the next command after the function call. Any command associated with the RETURN trap is executed before execution resumes. When a function completes, the values of the positional parameters and the special parameter '#' are restored to the values they had prior to the function's execution. If a numeric argument is given to `return`, that is the function's return status; otherwise the function's return status is the exit status of the last command executed before the `return`.

Variables local to the function may be declared with the `local` builtin. These variables are visible only to the function and the commands it invokes.

Function names and definitions may be listed with the `-f` option to the `declare` (`typeset`) builtin command (see Section 4.2 [Bash Builtins], page 49). The `-F` option to `declare` or `typeset` will list the function names only (and optionally the source file and line number, if the `extdebug` shell option is enabled). Functions may be exported so that subshells automatically have them defined with the `-f` option to the `export` builtin (see Section 4.1 [Bourne Shell Builtins], page 42). Note that shell functions and variables with the same name may result in multiple identically-named entries in the environment passed to the shell's children. Care should be taken in cases where this may cause a problem.

Functions may be recursive. The FUNCNEST variable may be used to limit the depth of the function call stack and restrict the number of function invocations. By default, no limit is placed on the number of recursive calls.

3.4 Shell Parameters

A *parameter* is an entity that stores values. It can be a `name`, a number, or one of the special characters listed below. A *variable* is a parameter denoted by a `name`. A variable has a *value* and zero or more *attributes*. Attributes are assigned using the `declare` builtin command (see the description of the `declare` builtin in Section 4.2 [Bash Builtins], page 49).

A parameter is set if it has been assigned a value. The null string is a valid value. Once a variable is set, it may be unset only by using the `unset` builtin command.

A variable may be assigned to by a statement of the form

        name=[*value*]

If *value* is not given, the variable is assigned the null string. All *values* undergo tilde expansion, parameter and variable expansion, command substitution, arithmetic expansion, and quote removal (detailed below). If the variable has its `integer` attribute set, then *value* is evaluated as an arithmetic expression even if the $((...)) expansion is not used (see Section 3.5.5 [Arithmetic Expansion], page 29). Word splitting is not performed, with the exception of "$@" as explained below. Filename expansion is not performed. Assignment statements may also appear as arguments to the **alias**, **declare**, **typeset**, **export**, **readonly**, and **local** builtin commands (*declaration* commands). When in POSIX mode (see Section 6.11 [Bash POSIX Mode], page 96), these builtins may appear in a command after one or more instances of the **command** builtin and retain these assignment statement properties.

In the context where an assignment statement is assigning a value to a shell variable or array index (see Section 6.7 [Arrays], page 91), the '+=' operator can be used to append to or add to the variable's previous value. This includes arguments to builtin commands such as **declare** that accept assignment statements (*declaration* commands). When '+=' is applied to a variable for which the *integer* attribute has been set, *value* is evaluated as an arithmetic expression and added to the variable's current value, which is also evaluated. When '+=' is applied to an array variable using compound assignment (see Section 6.7 [Arrays], page 91), the variable's value is not unset (as it is when using '='), and new values are appended to the array beginning at one greater than the array's maximum index (for indexed arrays), or added as additional key-value pairs in an associative array. When applied to a string-valued variable, *value* is expanded and appended to the variable's value.

A variable can be assigned the *nameref* attribute using the **-n** option to the **declare** or **local** builtin commands (see Section 4.2 [Bash Builtins], page 49) to create a *nameref*, or a reference to another variable. This allows variables to be manipulated indirectly. Whenever the nameref variable is referenced, assigned to, unset, or has its attributes modified (other than using or changing the nameref attribute itself), the operation is actually performed on the variable specified by the nameref variable's value. A nameref is commonly used within shell functions to refer to a variable whose name is passed as an argument to the function. For instance, if a variable name is passed to a shell function as its first argument, running

```
declare -n ref=$1
```

inside the function creates a nameref variable *ref* whose value is the variable name passed as the first argument. References and assignments to *ref*, and changes to its attributes, are treated as references, assignments, and attribute modifications to the variable whose name was passed as $1.

If the control variable in a **for** loop has the nameref attribute, the list of words can be a list of shell variables, and a name reference will be established for each word in the list, in turn, when the loop is executed. Array variables cannot be given the nameref attribute. However, nameref variables can reference array variables and subscripted array variables. Namerefs can be unset using the **-n** option to the **unset** builtin (see Section 4.1 [Bourne Shell Builtins], page 42). Otherwise, if **unset** is executed with the name of a nameref variable as an argument, the variable referenced by the nameref variable will be unset.

3.4.1 Positional Parameters

A *positional parameter* is a parameter denoted by one or more digits, other than the single digit 0. Positional parameters are assigned from the shell's arguments when it is invoked, and may be reassigned using the **set** builtin command. Positional parameter N may be referenced as ${N}, or as $N when N consists of a single digit. Positional parameters may not be assigned to with assignment statements. The **set** and **shift** builtins are used to set and unset them (see Chapter 4 [Shell Builtin Commands], page 42). The positional parameters are temporarily replaced when a shell function is executed (see Section 3.3 [Shell Functions], page 17).

When a positional parameter consisting of more than a single digit is expanded, it must be enclosed in braces.

3.4.2 Special Parameters

The shell treats several parameters specially. These parameters may only be referenced; assignment to them is not allowed.

*   ($*) Expands to the positional parameters, starting from one. When the expansion is not within double quotes, each positional parameter expands to a separate word. In contexts where it is performed, those words are subject to further word splitting and pathname expansion. When the expansion occurs within double quotes, it expands to a single word with the value of each parameter separated by the first character of the IFS special variable. That is, "$*" is equivalent to "$1c$2c...", where c is the first character of the value of the IFS variable. If IFS is unset, the parameters are separated by spaces. If IFS is null, the parameters are joined without intervening separators.

@   ($@) Expands to the positional parameters, starting from one. When the expansion occurs within double quotes, each parameter expands to a separate word. That is, "$@" is equivalent to "$1" "$2" .... If the double-quoted expansion occurs within a word, the expansion of the first parameter is joined with the beginning part of the original word, and the expansion of the last parameter is joined with the last part of the original word. When there are no positional parameters, "$@" and $@ expand to nothing (i.e., they are removed).

($#) Expands to the number of positional parameters in decimal.

?   ($?) Expands to the exit status of the most recently executed foreground pipeline.

-       ($-, a hyphen.) Expands to the current option flags as specified upon invocation, by the set builtin command, or those set by the shell itself (such as the -i option).

$ ($$) Expands to the process ID of the shell. In a () subshell, it expands to the process ID of the invoking shell, not the subshell.

!   ($!) Expands to the process ID of the job most recently placed into the background, whether executed as an asynchronous command or using the bg builtin (see Section 7.2 [Job Control Builtins], page 101).

0   ($0) Expands to the name of the shell or shell script. This is set at shell initialization. If Bash is invoked with a file of commands (see Section 3.8 [Shell Scripts], page 40), $0 is set to the name of that file. If Bash is started with the -c option (see Section 6.1 [Invoking Bash], page 82), then $0 is set to the first argument after the string to be executed, if one is present. Otherwise, it is set to the filename used to invoke Bash, as given by argument zero.

_   ($_, an underscore.) At shell startup, set to the absolute pathname used to invoke the shell or shell script being executed as passed in the environment or argument list. Subsequently, expands to the last argument to the previous command, after expansion. Also set to the full pathname used to invoke each command executed and placed in the environment exported to that command. When checking mail, this parameter holds the name of the mail file.

3.5 Shell Expansions

Expansion is performed on the command line after it has been split into `tokens`. There are seven kinds of expansion performed:

- brace expansion
- tilde expansion
- parameter and variable expansion
- command substitution
- arithmetic expansion
- word splitting
- filename expansion

The order of expansions is: brace expansion; tilde expansion, parameter and variable expansion, arithmetic expansion, and command substitution (done in a left-to-right fashion); word splitting; and filename expansion.

On systems that can support it, there is an additional expansion available: *process substitution*. This is performed at the same time as tilde, parameter, variable, and arithmetic expansion and command substitution.

After these expansions are performed, quote characters present in the original word are removed unless they have been quoted themselves (*quote removal*).

Only brace expansion, word splitting, and filename expansion can change the number of words of the expansion; other expansions expand a single word to a single word. The only exceptions to this are the expansions of `"$@"` (see Section 3.4.2 [Special Parameters], page 20) and `"${name[@]}"` (see Section 6.7 [Arrays], page 91).

After all expansions, `quote removal` (see Section 3.5.9 [Quote Removal], page 32) is performed.

3.5.1 Brace Expansion

Brace expansion is a mechanism by which arbitrary strings may be generated. This mechanism is similar to *filename expansion* (see Section 3.5.8 [Filename Expansion], page 30), but the filenames generated need not exist. Patterns to be brace expanded take the form of an optional *preamble*, followed by either a series of comma-separated strings or a sequence expression between a pair of braces, followed by an optional *postscript*. The preamble is prefixed to each string contained within the braces, and the postscript is then appended to each resulting string, expanding left to right.

Brace expansions may be nested. The results of each expanded string are not sorted; left to right order is preserved. For example,

```
bash$ echo a{d,c,b}e
ade ace abe
```

A sequence expression takes the form `{x..y[..incr]}`, where x and y are either integers or single characters, and *incr*, an optional increment, is an integer. When integers are supplied, the expression expands to each number between x and y, inclusive. Supplied integers may be prefixed with '0' to force each term to have the same width. When either x or y begins with a zero, the shell attempts to force all generated terms to contain the same number of digits, zero-padding where necessary. When characters are supplied, the expression expands to each character lexicographically between x and y, inclusive, using the default C locale. Note that both x and y must be of the same type. When the increment is supplied, it is used as the difference between each term. The default increment is 1 or -1 as appropriate.

Brace expansion is performed before any other expansions, and any characters special to other expansions are preserved in the result. It is strictly textual. Bash does not apply any syntactic interpretation to the context of the expansion or the text between the braces. To avoid conflicts with parameter expansion, the string '${' is not considered eligible for brace expansion.

A correctly-formed brace expansion must contain unquoted opening and closing braces, and at least one unquoted comma or a valid sequence expression. Any incorrectly formed brace expansion is left unchanged.

A { or ',' may be quoted with a backslash to prevent its being considered part of a brace expression. To avoid conflicts with parameter expansion, the string '${' is not considered eligible for brace expansion.

This construct is typically used as shorthand when the common prefix of the strings to be generated is longer than in the above example:

```
mkdir /usr/local/src/bash/{old,new,dist,bugs}
```

or

```
chown root /usr/{ucb/{ex,edit},lib/{ex?.?*,how_ex}}
```

3.5.2 Tilde Expansion

If a word begins with an unquoted tilde character ('~'), all of the characters up to the first unquoted slash (or all characters, if there is no unquoted slash) are considered a *tilde-prefix*. If none of the characters in the tilde-prefix are quoted, the characters in the tilde-prefix following the tilde are treated as a possible *login name*. If this login name is the null string, the tilde is replaced with the value of the HOME shell variable. If HOME is unset, the home directory of the user executing the shell is substituted instead. Otherwise, the tilde-prefix is replaced with the home directory associated with the specified login name.

If the tilde-prefix is '~+', the value of the shell variable PWD replaces the tilde-prefix. If the tilde-prefix is '~-', the value of the shell variable OLDPWD, if it is set, is substituted.

If the characters following the tilde in the tilde-prefix consist of a number N, optionally prefixed by a '+' or a '-', the tilde-prefix is replaced with the corresponding element from the directory stack, as it would be displayed by the `dirs` builtin invoked with the characters following tilde in the tilde-prefix as an argument (see Section 6.8 [The Directory Stack], page 93). If the tilde-prefix, sans the tilde, consists of a number without a leading '+' or '-', '+' is assumed.

If the login name is invalid, or the tilde expansion fails, the word is left unchanged.

Each variable assignment is checked for unquoted tilde-prefixes immediately following a ':' or the first '='. In these cases, tilde expansion is also performed. Consequently, one may use filenames with tildes in assignments to PATH, MAILPATH, and CDPATH, and the shell assigns the expanded value.

The following table shows how Bash treats unquoted tilde-prefixes:

~	The value of $HOME
~/foo	$HOME/foo
~fred/foo	The subdirectory foo of the home directory of the user fred
~+/foo	$PWD/foo
~-/foo	${OLDPWD-'~-'}/foo
~N	The string that would be displayed by 'dirs +N'
~+N	The string that would be displayed by 'dirs +N'
~-N	The string that would be displayed by 'dirs -N'

3.5.3 Shell Parameter Expansion

The '$' character introduces parameter expansion, command substitution, or arithmetic expansion. The parameter name or symbol to be expanded may be enclosed in braces, which are optional but serve to protect the variable to be expanded from characters immediately following it which could be interpreted as part of the name.

When braces are used, the matching ending brace is the first '}' not escaped by a backslash or within a quoted string, and not within an embedded arithmetic expansion, command substitution, or parameter expansion.

The basic form of parameter expansion is ${parameter}. The value of parameter is substituted. The parameter is a shell parameter as described above (see Section 3.4 [Shell Parameters], page 18) or an array reference (see Section 6.7 [Arrays], page 91). The braces are required when parameter is a positional parameter with more than one digit, or when parameter is followed by a character that is not to be interpreted as part of its name.

If the first character of parameter is an exclamation point (!), and parameter is not a nameref, it introduces a level of variable indirection. Bash uses the value of the variable formed from the rest of parameter as the name of the variable; this variable is then expanded and that value is used in the rest of the substitution, rather than the value of parameter itself. This is known as **indirect expansion**. If parameter is a nameref, this expands to the name of the variable referenced by parameter instead of performing the complete indirect expansion. The exceptions to this are the expansions of ${!prefix*} and ${!name[@]} described below. The exclamation point must immediately follow the left brace in order to introduce indirection.

In each of the cases below, word is subject to tilde expansion, parameter expansion, command substitution, and arithmetic expansion.

When not performing substring expansion, using the form described below (e.g., ':-'), Bash tests for a parameter that is unset or null. Omitting the colon results in a test only for a parameter that is unset. Put another way, if the colon is included, the operator tests for both *parameter*'s existence and that its value is not null; if the colon is omitted, the operator tests only for existence.

${*parameter*:−*word*}

        If *parameter* is unset or null, the expansion of *word* is substituted. Otherwise, the value of *parameter* is substituted.

${*parameter*:=*word*}

        If *parameter* is unset or null, the expansion of *word* is assigned to *parameter*. The value of *parameter* is then substituted. Positional parameters and special parameters may not be assigned to in this way.

${*parameter*:?*word*}

        If *parameter* is null or unset, the expansion of *word* (or a message to that effect if *word* is not present) is written to the standard error and the shell, if it is not interactive, exits. Otherwise, the value of *parameter* is substituted.

${*parameter*:+*word*}

        If *parameter* is null or unset, nothing is substituted, otherwise the expansion of *word* is substituted.

${*parameter*:*offset*}

${*parameter*:*offset*:*length*}

        This is referred to as Substring Expansion. It expands to up to *length* characters of the value of *parameter* starting at the character specified by *offset*. If *parameter* is '@', an indexed array subscripted by '@' or '*', or an associative array name, the results differ as described below. If *length* is omitted, it expands to the substring of the value of *parameter* starting at the character specified by *offset* and extending to the end of the value. *length* and *offset* are arithmetic expressions (see Section 6.5 [Shell Arithmetic], page 89).

        If *offset* evaluates to a number less than zero, the value is used as an offset in characters from the end of the value of *parameter*. If *length* evaluates to a number less than zero, it is interpreted as an offset in characters from the end of the value of *parameter* rather than a number of characters, and the expansion is the characters between *offset* and that result. Note that a negative offset must be separated from the colon by at least one space to avoid being confused with the ':-' expansion.

        Here are some examples illustrating substring expansion on parameters and subscripted arrays:

```
$ string=01234567890abcdefgh
$ echo ${string:7}
7890abcdefgh
$ echo ${string:7:0}

$ echo ${string:7:2}
78
$ echo ${string:7:-2}
7890abcdef
$ echo ${string: -7}
```

```
bcdefgh
$ echo ${string: -7:0}

$ echo ${string: -7:2}
bc
$ echo ${string: -7:-2}
bcdef
$ set -- 01234567890abcdefgh
$ echo ${1:7}
7890abcdefgh
$ echo ${1:7:0}

$ echo ${1:7:2}
78
$ echo ${1:7:-2}
7890abcdef
$ echo ${1: -7}
bcdefgh
$ echo ${1: -7:0}

$ echo ${1: -7:2}
bc
$ echo ${1: -7:-2}
bcdef
$ array[0]=01234567890abcdefgh
$ echo ${array[0]:7}
7890abcdefgh
$ echo ${array[0]:7:0}

$ echo ${array[0]:7:2}
78
$ echo ${array[0]:7:-2}
7890abcdef
$ echo ${array[0]: -7}
bcdefgh
$ echo ${array[0]: -7:0}

$ echo ${array[0]: -7:2}
bc
$ echo ${array[0]: -7:-2}
bcdef
```

If *parameter* is '@', the result is *length* positional parameters beginning at *offset*. A negative *offset* is taken relative to one greater than the greatest positional parameter, so an offset of -1 evaluates to the last positional parameter. It is an expansion error if *length* evaluates to a number less than zero.

The following examples illustrate substring expansion using positional parameters:

```
$ set -- 1 2 3 4 5 6 7 8 9 0 a b c d e f g h
$ echo ${@:7}
7 8 9 0 a b c d e f g h
$ echo ${@:7:0}

$ echo ${@:7:2}
7 8
$ echo ${@:7:-2}
bash: -2: substring expression < 0
$ echo ${@: -7:2}
b c
$ echo ${@:0}
./bash 1 2 3 4 5 6 7 8 9 0 a b c d e f g h
$ echo ${@:0:2}
./bash 1
$ echo ${@: -7:0}
```

If *parameter* is an indexed array name subscripted by '@' or '*', the result is the *length* members of the array beginning with ${*parameter*[*offset*]}. A negative *offset* is taken relative to one greater than the maximum index of the specified array. It is an expansion error if *length* evaluates to a number less than zero.

These examples show how you can use substring expansion with indexed arrays:

```
$ array=(0 1 2 3 4 5 6 7 8 9 0 a b c d e f g h)
$ echo ${array[@]:7}
7 8 9 0 a b c d e f g h
$ echo ${array[@]:7:2}
7 8
$ echo ${array[@]: -7:2}
b c
$ echo ${array[@]: -7:-2}
bash: -2: substring expression < 0
$ echo ${array[@]:0}
0 1 2 3 4 5 6 7 8 9 0 a b c d e f g h
$ echo ${array[@]:0:2}
0 1
$ echo ${array[@]: -7:0}
```

Substring expansion applied to an associative array produces undefined results.

Substring indexing is zero-based unless the positional parameters are used, in which case the indexing starts at 1 by default. If *offset* is 0, and the positional parameters are used, $@ is prefixed to the list.

`${!prefix*}`
`${!prefix@}`

> Expands to the names of variables whose names begin with *prefix*, separated by the first character of the IFS special variable. When '@' is used and the expansion appears within double quotes, each variable name expands to a separate word.

`${!name[@]}`
`${!name[*]}`

> If *name* is an array variable, expands to the list of array indices (keys) assigned in *name*. If *name* is not an array, expands to 0 if *name* is set and null otherwise. When '@' is used and the expansion appears within double quotes, each key expands to a separate word.

`${#parameter}`

> The length in characters of the expanded value of *parameter* is substituted. If *parameter* is '*' or '@', the value substituted is the number of positional parameters. If *parameter* is an array name subscripted by '*' or '@', the value substituted is the number of elements in the array. If *parameter* is an indexed array name subscripted by a negative number, that number is interpreted as relative to one greater than the maximum index of *parameter*, so negative indices count back from the end of the array, and an index of -1 references the last element.

`${parameter#word}`
`${parameter##word}`

> The *word* is expanded to produce a pattern just as in filename expansion (see Section 3.5.8 [Filename Expansion], page 30). If the pattern matches the beginning of the expanded value of *parameter*, then the result of the expansion is the expanded value of *parameter* with the shortest matching pattern (the '#' case) or the longest matching pattern (the '##' case) deleted. If *parameter* is '@' or '*', the pattern removal operation is applied to each positional parameter in turn, and the expansion is the resultant list. If *parameter* is an array variable subscripted with '@' or '*', the pattern removal operation is applied to each member of the array in turn, and the expansion is the resultant list.

`${parameter%word}`
`${parameter%%word}`

> The *word* is expanded to produce a pattern just as in filename expansion. If the pattern matches a trailing portion of the expanded value of *parameter*, then the result of the expansion is the value of *parameter* with the shortest matching pattern (the '%' case) or the longest matching pattern (the '%%' case) deleted. If *parameter* is '@' or '*', the pattern removal operation is applied to each positional parameter in turn, and the expansion is the resultant list. If *parameter* is an array variable subscripted with '@' or '*', the pattern removal operation is applied to each member of the array in turn, and the expansion is the resultant list.

`${parameter/pattern/string}`

> The *pattern* is expanded to produce a pattern just as in filename expansion. *Parameter* is expanded and the longest match of *pattern* against its value is replaced with *string*. If *pattern* begins with '/', all matches of *pattern* are replaced with *string*. Normally only the first match is replaced. If *pattern* begins with '#', it must match at the beginning of the expanded value of *parameter*. If *pattern* begins with '%', it must match at the end of the expanded value of *parameter*. If *string* is null, matches of *pattern* are deleted and the / following *pattern* may be omitted. If the `nocasematch` shell option (see the description of `shopt` in Section 4.3.2 [The Shopt Builtin], page 64) is enabled, the match is performed without regard to the case of alphabetic characters. If *parameter* is '@' or '*', the substitution operation is applied to each positional parameter in turn, and the expansion is the resultant list. If *parameter* is an array variable subscripted with '@' or '*', the substitution operation is applied to each member of the array in turn, and the expansion is the resultant list.

`${parameter^pattern}`
`${parameter^^pattern}`
`${parameter,pattern}`
`${parameter,,pattern}`

> This expansion modifies the case of alphabetic characters in *parameter*. The *pattern* is expanded to produce a pattern just as in filename expansion. Each character in the expanded value of *parameter* is tested against *pattern*, and, if it matches the pattern, its case is converted. The pattern should not attempt to match more than one character. The '^' operator converts lowercase letters matching *pattern* to uppercase; the ',' operator converts matching uppercase letters to lowercase. The '^^' and ',,' expansions convert each matched character in the expanded value; the '^' and ',' expansions match and convert only the first character in the expanded value. If *pattern* is omitted, it is treated like a '?', which matches every character. If *parameter* is '@' or '*', the case modification operation is applied to each positional parameter in turn, and the expansion is the resultant list. If *parameter* is an array variable subscripted with '@' or '*', the case modification operation is applied to each member of the array in turn, and the expansion is the resultant list.

`${parameter@operator}`

> The expansion is either a transformation of the value of *parameter* or information about *parameter* itself, depending on the value of *operator*. Each *operator* is a single letter:

> Q   The expansion is a string that is the value of *parameter* quoted in a format that can be reused as input.

> E   The expansion is a string that is the value of *parameter* with backslash escape sequences expanded as with the `$'...'` quoting mechansim.

> P   The expansion is a string that is the result of expanding the value of *parameter* as if it were a prompt string (see Section 6.9 [Controlling the Prompt], page 94).

A   The expansion is a string in the form of an assignment statement or `declare` command that, if evaluated, will recreate *parameter* with its attributes and value.

a   The expansion is a string consisting of flag values representing *parameter*'s attributes.

If *parameter* is '`@`' or '`*`', the operation is applied to each positional parameter in turn, and the expansion is the resultant list. If *parameter* is an array variable subscripted with '`@`' or '`*`', the operation is applied to each member of the array in turn, and the expansion is the resultant list.

The result of the expansion is subject to word splitting and pathname expansion as described below.

3.5.4 Command Substitution

Command substitution allows the output of a command to replace the command itself. Command substitution occurs when a command is enclosed as follows:

```
$(command)
```

or

```
`command`
```

Bash performs the expansion by executing *command* in a subshell environment and replacing the command substitution with the standard output of the command, with any trailing newlines deleted. Embedded newlines are not deleted, but they may be removed during word splitting. The command substitution `$(cat file)` can be replaced by the equivalent but faster `$(< file)`.

When the old-style backquote form of substitution is used, backslash retains its literal meaning except when followed by '`$`', '`` ` ``', or '`\`'. The first backquote not preceded by a backslash terminates the command substitution. When using the `$(command)` form, all characters between the parentheses make up the command; none are treated specially.

Command substitutions may be nested. To nest when using the backquoted form, escape the inner backquotes with backslashes.

If the substitution appears within double quotes, word splitting and filename expansion are not performed on the results.

3.5.5 Arithmetic Expansion

Arithmetic expansion allows the evaluation of an arithmetic expression and the substitution of the result. The format for arithmetic expansion is:

```
$(( expression ))
```

The expression is treated as if it were within double quotes, but a double quote inside the parentheses is not treated specially. All tokens in the expression undergo parameter and variable expansion, command substitution, and quote removal. The result is treated as the arithmetic expression to be evaluated. Arithmetic expansions may be nested.

The evaluation is performed according to the rules listed below (see Section 6.5 [Shell Arithmetic], page 89). If the expression is invalid, Bash prints a message indicating failure to the standard error and no substitution occurs.

3.5.6 Process Substitution

Process substitution allows a process's input or output to be referred to using a filename. It takes the form of

        <(*list*)

or

        >(*list*)

The process *list* is run asynchronously, and its input or output appears as a filename. This filename is passed as an argument to the current command as the result of the expansion. If the >(*list*) form is used, writing to the file will provide input for *list*. If the <(*list*) form is used, the file passed as an argument should be read to obtain the output of *list*. Note that no space may appear between the < or > and the left parenthesis, otherwise the construct would be interpreted as a redirection. Process substitution is supported on systems that support named pipes (FIFOs) or the /dev/fd method of naming open files.

When available, process substitution is performed simultaneously with parameter and variable expansion, command substitution, and arithmetic expansion.

3.5.7 Word Splitting

The shell scans the results of parameter expansion, command substitution, and arithmetic expansion that did not occur within double quotes for word splitting.

The shell treats each character of $IFS as a delimiter, and splits the results of the other expansions into words using these characters as field terminators. If IFS is unset, or its value is exactly <space><tab><newline>, the default, then sequences of <space>, <tab>, and <newline> at the beginning and end of the results of the previous expansions are ignored, and any sequence of IFS characters not at the beginning or end serves to delimit words. If IFS has a value other than the default, then sequences of the whitespace characters space, tab, and newline are ignored at the beginning and end of the word, as long as the whitespace character is in the value of IFS (an IFS whitespace character). Any character in IFS that is not IFS whitespace, along with any adjacent IFS whitespace characters, delimits a field. A sequence of IFS whitespace characters is also treated as a delimiter. If the value of IFS is null, no word splitting occurs.

Explicit null arguments ("" or '') are retained and passed to commands as empty strings. Unquoted implicit null arguments, resulting from the expansion of parameters that have no values, are removed. If a parameter with no value is expanded within double quotes, a null argument results and is retained and passed to a command as an empty string. When a quoted null argument appears as part of a word whose expansion is non-null, the null argument is removed. That is, the word -d'' becomes -d after word splitting and null argument removal.

Note that if no expansion occurs, no splitting is performed.

3.5.8 Filename Expansion

After word splitting, unless the -f option has been set (see Section 4.3.1 [The Set Builtin], page 60), Bash scans each word for the characters '*', '?', and '['. If one of these characters appears, then the word is regarded as a *pattern*, and replaced with an alphabetically sorted list of filenames matching the pattern (see Section 3.5.8.1 [Pattern Matching], page 31). If no matching filenames are found, and the shell option `nullglob` is disabled, the word is left unchanged. If the `nullglob` option is set, and no matches are found, the word is removed. If the `failglob` shell option is set, and no matches are found, an error message is printed and the command is not executed. If the shell option `nocaseglob` is enabled, the match is performed without regard to the case of alphabetic characters.

When a pattern is used for filename expansion, the character '.' at the start of a filename or immediately following a slash must be matched explicitly, unless the shell option `dotglob` is set. When matching a filename, the slash character must always be matched explicitly. In other cases, the '.' character is not treated specially.

See the description of `shopt` in Section 4.3.2 [The Shopt Builtin], page 64, for a description of the `nocaseglob`, `nullglob`, `failglob`, and `dotglob` options.

The `GLOBIGNORE` shell variable may be used to restrict the set of filenames matching a pattern. If `GLOBIGNORE` is set, each matching filename that also matches one of the patterns in `GLOBIGNORE` is removed from the list of matches. If the `nocaseglob` option is set, the matching against the patterns in `GLOBIGNORE` is performed without regard to case. The filenames . and .. are always ignored when `GLOBIGNORE` is set and not null. However, setting `GLOBIGNORE` to a non-null value has the effect of enabling the `dotglob` shell option, so all other filenames beginning with a '.' will match. To get the old behavior of ignoring filenames beginning with a '.', make '.*' one of the patterns in `GLOBIGNORE`. The `dotglob` option is disabled when `GLOBIGNORE` is unset.

3.5.8.1 Pattern Matching

Any character that appears in a pattern, other than the special pattern characters described below, matches itself. The NUL character may not occur in a pattern. A backslash escapes the following character; the escaping backslash is discarded when matching. The special pattern characters must be quoted if they are to be matched literally.

The special pattern characters have the following meanings:

*   Matches any string, including the null string. When the `globstar` shell option is enabled, and '*' is used in a filename expansion context, two adjacent '*'s used as a single pattern will match all files and zero or more directories and subdirectories. If followed by a '/', two adjacent '*'s will match only directories and subdirectories.

?   Matches any single character.

[...]   Matches any one of the enclosed characters. A pair of characters separated by a hyphen denotes a *range expression*; any character that falls between those two characters, inclusive, using the current locale's collating sequence and character set, is matched. If the first character following the '[' is a '!' or a '^' then any character not enclosed is matched. A '−' may be matched by including it as the first or last character in the set. A ']' may be matched by including it as the first character in the set. The sorting order of characters in range expressions is determined by the current locale and the values of the `LC_COLLATE` and `LC_ALL` shell variables, if set.

For example, in the default C locale, '[a-dx-z]' is equivalent to '[abcdxyz]'. Many locales sort characters in dictionary order, and in these locales '[a-dx-z]' is typically not equivalent to '[abcdxyz]'; it might be equivalent to '[aBbCcDdxXyYz]', for example. To obtain the traditional interpretation of ranges in bracket expressions, you can force the use of the C locale by setting the LC_COLLATE or LC_ALL environment variable to the value 'C', or enable the globasciiranges shell option.

Within '[' and ']', *character classes* can be specified using the syntax [:*class*:], where *class* is one of the following classes defined in the POSIX standard:

| alnum | alpha | ascii | blank | cntrl | digit | graph | lower |
| print | punct | space | upper | word | xdigit | | |

A character class matches any character belonging to that class. The word character class matches letters, digits, and the character '_'.

Within '[' and ']', an *equivalence class* can be specified using the syntax [=*c*=], which matches all characters with the same collation weight (as defined by the current locale) as the character *c*.

Within '[' and ']', the syntax [.*symbol*.] matches the collating symbol *symbol*.

If the extglob shell option is enabled using the shopt builtin, several extended pattern matching operators are recognized. In the following description, a *pattern-list* is a list of one or more patterns separated by a '|'. Composite patterns may be formed using one or more of the following sub-patterns:

?(*pattern-list*)
> Matches zero or one occurrence of the given patterns.

*(*pattern-list*)
> Matches zero or more occurrences of the given patterns.

+(*pattern-list*)
> Matches one or more occurrences of the given patterns.

@(*pattern-list*)
> Matches one of the given patterns.

!(*pattern-list*)
> Matches anything except one of the given patterns.

3.5.9 Quote Removal

After the preceding expansions, all unquoted occurrences of the characters '\', ''', and '"' that did not result from one of the above expansions are removed.

3.6 Redirections

Before a command is executed, its input and output may be *redirected* using a special notation interpreted by the shell. Redirection allows commands' file handles to be duplicated, opened, closed, made to refer to different files, and can change the files the command reads from and writes to. Redirection may also be used to modify file handles in the current shell execution environment. The following redirection operators may precede or appear anywhere within a simple command or may follow a command. Redirections are processed in the order they appear, from left to right.

Each redirection that may be preceded by a file descriptor number may instead be preceded by a word of the form {*varname*}. In this case, for each redirection operator except >&- and <&-, the shell will allocate a file descriptor greater than 10 and assign it to {*varname*}. If >&- or <&- is preceded by {*varname*}, the value of *varname* defines the file descriptor to close.

In the following descriptions, if the file descriptor number is omitted, and the first character of the redirection operator is '<', the redirection refers to the standard input (file descriptor 0). If the first character of the redirection operator is '>', the redirection refers to the standard output (file descriptor 1).

The word following the redirection operator in the following descriptions, unless otherwise noted, is subjected to brace expansion, tilde expansion, parameter expansion, command substitution, arithmetic expansion, quote removal, filename expansion, and word splitting. If it expands to more than one word, Bash reports an error.

Note that the order of redirections is significant. For example, the command

```
ls > dirlist 2>&1
```

directs both standard output (file descriptor 1) and standard error (file descriptor 2) to the file *dirlist*, while the command

```
ls 2>&1 > dirlist
```

directs only the standard output to file *dirlist*, because the standard error was made a copy of the standard output before the standard output was redirected to *dirlist*.

Bash handles several filenames specially when they are used in redirections, as described in the following table. If the operating system on which Bash is running provides these special files, bash will use them; otherwise it will emulate them internally with the behavior described below.

`/dev/fd/fd`
> If *fd* is a valid integer, file descriptor *fd* is duplicated.

`/dev/stdin`
> File descriptor 0 is duplicated.

`/dev/stdout`
> File descriptor 1 is duplicated.

`/dev/stderr`
> File descriptor 2 is duplicated.

`/dev/tcp/host/port`
> If *host* is a valid hostname or Internet address, and *port* is an integer port number or service name, Bash attempts to open the corresponding TCP socket.

`/dev/udp/host/port`
> If *host* is a valid hostname or Internet address, and *port* is an integer port number or service name, Bash attempts to open the corresponding UDP socket.

A failure to open or create a file causes the redirection to fail.

Redirections using file descriptors greater than 9 should be used with care, as they may conflict with file descriptors the shell uses internally.

3.6.1 Redirecting Input

Redirection of input causes the file whose name results from the expansion of *word* to be opened for reading on file descriptor **n**, or the standard input (file descriptor 0) if **n** is not specified.

The general format for redirecting input is:

    [n]<word

3.6.2 Redirecting Output

Redirection of output causes the file whose name results from the expansion of *word* to be opened for writing on file descriptor *n*, or the standard output (file descriptor 1) if *n* is not specified. If the file does not exist it is created; if it does exist it is truncated to zero size.

The general format for redirecting output is:

    [n]>[|] word

If the redirection operator is '>', and the `noclobber` option to the `set` builtin has been enabled, the redirection will fail if the file whose name results from the expansion of *word* exists and is a regular file. If the redirection operator is '>|', or the redirection operator is '>' and the `noclobber` option is not enabled, the redirection is attempted even if the file named by *word* exists.

3.6.3 Appending Redirected Output

Redirection of output in this fashion causes the file whose name results from the expansion of *word* to be opened for appending on file descriptor *n*, or the standard output (file descriptor 1) if *n* is not specified. If the file does not exist it is created.

The general format for appending output is:

    [n]>>word

3.6.4 Redirecting Standard Output and Standard Error

This construct allows both the standard output (file descriptor 1) and the standard error output (file descriptor 2) to be redirected to the file whose name is the expansion of *word*.

There are two formats for redirecting standard output and standard error:

    &>word

and

    >&word

Of the two forms, the first is preferred. This is semantically equivalent to

    >word 2>&1

When using the second form, *word* may not expand to a number or '-'. If it does, other redirection operators apply (see Duplicating File Descriptors below) for compatibility reasons.

3.6.5 Appending Standard Output and Standard Error

This construct allows both the standard output (file descriptor 1) and the standard error output (file descriptor 2) to be appended to the file whose name is the expansion of *word*.

The format for appending standard output and standard error is:

```
&>>word
```

This is semantically equivalent to

```
>>word 2>&1
```

(see Duplicating File Descriptors below).

3.6.6 Here Documents

This type of redirection instructs the shell to read input from the current source until a line containing only *word* (with no trailing blanks) is seen. All of the lines read up to that point are then used as the standard input (or file descriptor *n* if *n* is specified) for a command.

The format of here-documents is:

```
[n]<<[−]word
        here-document
delimiter
```

No parameter and variable expansion, command substitution, arithmetic expansion, or filename expansion is performed on *word*. If any part of *word* is quoted, the *delimiter* is the result of quote removal on *word*, and the lines in the here-document are not expanded. If *word* is unquoted, all lines of the here-document are subjected to parameter expansion, command substitution, and arithmetic expansion, the character sequence \newline is ignored, and '\' must be used to quote the characters '\', '$', and '`'.

If the redirection operator is '<<-', then all leading tab characters are stripped from input lines and the line containing *delimiter*. This allows here-documents within shell scripts to be indented in a natural fashion.

3.6.7 Here Strings

A variant of here documents, the format is:

```
[n]<<< word
```

The *word* undergoes brace expansion, tilde expansion, parameter and variable expansion, command substitution, arithmetic expansion, and quote removal. Pathname expansion and word splitting are not performed. The result is supplied as a single string, with a newline appended, to the command on its standard input (or file descriptor *n* if *n* is specified).

3.6.8 Duplicating File Descriptors

The redirection operator

```
[n]<&word
```

is used to duplicate input file descriptors. If *word* expands to one or more digits, the file descriptor denoted by *n* is made to be a copy of that file descriptor. If the digits in *word* do not specify a file descriptor open for input, a redirection error occurs. If *word* evaluates to '−', file descriptor *n* is closed. If *n* is not specified, the standard input (file descriptor 0) is used.

The operator

```
[n]>&word
```

is used similarly to duplicate output file descriptors. If *n* is not specified, the standard output (file descriptor 1) is used. If the digits in *word* do not specify a file descriptor open for output, a redirection error occurs. If *word* evaluates to '−', file descriptor *n* is closed. As a special case, if *n* is omitted, and *word* does not expand to one or more digits or '−', the standard output and standard error are redirected as described previously.

3.6.9 Moving File Descriptors

The redirection operator

```
[n]<&digit-
```

moves the file descriptor *digit* to file descriptor *n*, or the standard input (file descriptor 0) if *n* is not specified. *digit* is closed after being duplicated to *n*.

Similarly, the redirection operator

```
[n]>&digit-
```

moves the file descriptor *digit* to file descriptor *n*, or the standard output (file descriptor 1) if *n* is not specified.

3.6.10 Opening File Descriptors for Reading and Writing

The redirection operator

```
[n]<>word
```

causes the file whose name is the expansion of *word* to be opened for both reading and writing on file descriptor *n*, or on file descriptor 0 if *n* is not specified. If the file does not exist, it is created.

3.7 Executing Commands

3.7.1 Simple Command Expansion

When a simple command is executed, the shell performs the following expansions, assignments, and redirections, from left to right.

1. The words that the parser has marked as variable assignments (those preceding the command name) and redirections are saved for later processing.

2. The words that are not variable assignments or redirections are expanded (see Section 3.5 [Shell Expansions], page 21). If any words remain after expansion, the first word is taken to be the name of the command and the remaining words are the arguments.

3. Redirections are performed as described above (see Section 3.6 [Redirections], page 32).

4. The text after the '=' in each variable assignment undergoes tilde expansion, parameter expansion, command substitution, arithmetic expansion, and quote removal before being assigned to the variable.

If no command name results, the variable assignments affect the current shell environment. Otherwise, the variables are added to the environment of the executed command and do not affect the current shell environment. If any of the assignments attempts to assign a value to a readonly variable, an error occurs, and the command exits with a non-zero status.

If no command name results, redirections are performed, but do not affect the current shell environment. A redirection error causes the command to exit with a non-zero status.

If there is a command name left after expansion, execution proceeds as described below. Otherwise, the command exits. If one of the expansions contained a command substitution, the exit status of the command is the exit status of the last command substitution performed. If there were no command substitutions, the command exits with a status of zero.

3.7.2 Command Search and Execution

After a command has been split into words, if it results in a simple command and an optional list of arguments, the following actions are taken.

1. If the command name contains no slashes, the shell attempts to locate it. If there exists a shell function by that name, that function is invoked as described in Section 3.3 [Shell Functions], page 17.

2. If the name does not match a function, the shell searches for it in the list of shell builtins. If a match is found, that builtin is invoked.

3. If the name is neither a shell function nor a builtin, and contains no slashes, Bash searches each element of $PATH for a directory containing an executable file by that name. Bash uses a hash table to remember the full pathnames of executable files to avoid multiple PATH searches (see the description of hash in Section 4.1 [Bourne Shell Builtins], page 42). A full search of the directories in $PATH is performed only if the command is not found in the hash table. If the search is unsuccessful, the shell searches for a defined shell function named command_not_found_handle. If that function exists, it is invoked with the original command and the original command's arguments as its arguments, and the function's exit status becomes the exit status of the shell. If that function is not defined, the shell prints an error message and returns an exit status of 127.

4. If the search is successful, or if the command name contains one or more slashes, the shell executes the named program in a separate execution environment. Argument 0 is set to the name given, and the remaining arguments to the command are set to the arguments supplied, if any.

5. If this execution fails because the file is not in executable format, and the file is not a directory, it is assumed to be a *shell script* and the shell executes it as described in Section 3.8 [Shell Scripts], page 40.

6. If the command was not begun asynchronously, the shell waits for the command to complete and collects its exit status.

3.7.3 Command Execution Environment

The shell has an *execution environment*, which consists of the following:

- open files inherited by the shell at invocation, as modified by redirections supplied to the exec builtin

- the current working directory as set by cd, pushd, or popd, or inherited by the shell at invocation

- the file creation mode mask as set by umask or inherited from the shell's parent

- current traps set by `trap`
- shell parameters that are set by variable assignment or with `set` or inherited from the shell's parent in the environment
- shell functions defined during execution or inherited from the shell's parent in the environment
- options enabled at invocation (either by default or with command-line arguments) or by `set`
- options enabled by `shopt` (see Section 4.3.2 [The Shopt Builtin], page 64)
- shell aliases defined with `alias` (see Section 6.6 [Aliases], page 90)
- various process IDs, including those of background jobs (see Section 3.2.3 [Lists], page 9), the value of $$, and the value of $PPID

When a simple command other than a builtin or shell function is to be executed, it is invoked in a separate execution environment that consists of the following. Unless otherwise noted, the values are inherited from the shell.

- the shell's open files, plus any modifications and additions specified by redirections to the command
- the current working directory
- the file creation mode mask
- shell variables and functions marked for export, along with variables exported for the command, passed in the environment (see Section 3.7.4 [Environment], page 38)
- traps caught by the shell are reset to the values inherited from the shell's parent, and traps ignored by the shell are ignored

A command invoked in this separate environment cannot affect the shell's execution environment.

Command substitution, commands grouped with parentheses, and asynchronous commands are invoked in a subshell environment that is a duplicate of the shell environment, except that traps caught by the shell are reset to the values that the shell inherited from its parent at invocation. Builtin commands that are invoked as part of a pipeline are also executed in a subshell environment. Changes made to the subshell environment cannot affect the shell's execution environment.

Subshells spawned to execute command substitutions inherit the value of the `-e` option from the parent shell. When not in POSIX mode, Bash clears the `-e` option in such subshells.

If a command is followed by a '&' and job control is not active, the default standard input for the command is the empty file `/dev/null`. Otherwise, the invoked command inherits the file descriptors of the calling shell as modified by redirections.

3.7.4 Environment

When a program is invoked it is given an array of strings called the *environment*. This is a list of name-value pairs, of the form `name=value`.

Bash provides several ways to manipulate the environment. On invocation, the shell scans its own environment and creates a parameter for each name found, automatically marking it for *export* to child processes. Executed commands inherit the environment. The `export` and '`declare -x`' commands allow parameters and functions to be added to and deleted from the environment. If the value of a parameter in the environment is modified, the new value becomes part of the environment, replacing the old. The environment inherited by any executed command consists of the shell's initial environment, whose values may be modified in the shell, less any pairs removed by the **unset** and '`export -n`' commands, plus any additions via the **export** and '`declare -x`' commands.

The environment for any simple command or function may be augmented temporarily by prefixing it with parameter assignments, as described in Section 3.4 [Shell Parameters], page 18. These assignment statements affect only the environment seen by that command.

If the `-k` option is set (see Section 4.3.1 [The Set Builtin], page 60), then all parameter assignments are placed in the environment for a command, not just those that precede the command name.

When Bash invokes an external command, the variable '`$_`' is set to the full pathname of the command and passed to that command in its environment.

3.7.5 Exit Status

The exit status of an executed command is the value returned by the *waitpid* system call or equivalent function. Exit statuses fall between 0 and 255, though, as explained below, the shell may use values above 125 specially. Exit statuses from shell builtins and compound commands are also limited to this range. Under certain circumstances, the shell will use special values to indicate specific failure modes.

For the shell's purposes, a command which exits with a zero exit status has succeeded. A non-zero exit status indicates failure. This seemingly counter-intuitive scheme is used so there is one well-defined way to indicate success and a variety of ways to indicate various failure modes. When a command terminates on a fatal signal whose number is N, Bash uses the value $128+N$ as the exit status.

If a command is not found, the child process created to execute it returns a status of 127. If a command is found but is not executable, the return status is 126.

If a command fails because of an error during expansion or redirection, the exit status is greater than zero.

The exit status is used by the Bash conditional commands (see Section 3.2.4.2 [Conditional Constructs], page 10) and some of the list constructs (see Section 3.2.3 [Lists], page 9).

All of the Bash builtins return an exit status of zero if they succeed and a non-zero status on failure, so they may be used by the conditional and list constructs. All builtins return an exit status of 2 to indicate incorrect usage, generally invalid options or missing arguments.

3.7.6 Signals

When Bash is interactive, in the absence of any traps, it ignores SIGTERM (so that '`kill 0`' does not kill an interactive shell), and SIGINT is caught and handled (so that the **wait** builtin is interruptible). When Bash receives a SIGINT, it breaks out of any executing loops. In all cases, Bash ignores SIGQUIT. If job control is in effect (see Chapter 7 [Job Control], page 100), Bash ignores SIGTTIN, SIGTTOU, and SIGTSTP.

Non-builtin commands started by Bash have signal handlers set to the values inherited by the shell from its parent. When job control is not in effect, asynchronous commands ignore `SIGINT` and `SIGQUIT` in addition to these inherited handlers. Commands run as a result of command substitution ignore the keyboard-generated job control signals `SIGTTIN`, `SIGTTOU`, and `SIGTSTP`.

The shell exits by default upon receipt of a `SIGHUP`. Before exiting, an interactive shell resends the `SIGHUP` to all jobs, running or stopped. Stopped jobs are sent `SIGCONT` to ensure that they receive the `SIGHUP`. To prevent the shell from sending the `SIGHUP` signal to a particular job, it should be removed from the jobs table with the `disown` builtin (see Section 7.2 [Job Control Builtins], page 101) or marked to not receive `SIGHUP` using `disown -h`.

If the `huponexit` shell option has been set with `shopt` (see Section 4.3.2 [The Shopt Builtin], page 64), Bash sends a `SIGHUP` to all jobs when an interactive login shell exits.

If Bash is waiting for a command to complete and receives a signal for which a trap has been set, the trap will not be executed until the command completes. When Bash is waiting for an asynchronous command via the `wait` builtin, the reception of a signal for which a trap has been set will cause the `wait` builtin to return immediately with an exit status greater than 128, immediately after which the trap is executed.

3.8 Shell Scripts

A shell script is a text file containing shell commands. When such a file is used as the first non-option argument when invoking Bash, and neither the `-c` nor `-s` option is supplied (see Section 6.1 [Invoking Bash], page 82), Bash reads and executes commands from the file, then exits. This mode of operation creates a non-interactive shell. The shell first searches for the file in the current directory, and looks in the directories in `$PATH` if not found there.

When Bash runs a shell script, it sets the special parameter 0 to the name of the file, rather than the name of the shell, and the positional parameters are set to the remaining arguments, if any are given. If no additional arguments are supplied, the positional parameters are unset.

A shell script may be made executable by using the `chmod` command to turn on the execute bit. When Bash finds such a file while searching the `$PATH` for a command, it spawns a subshell to execute it. In other words, executing

        `filename` *arguments*

is equivalent to executing

        `bash filename` *arguments*

if `filename` is an executable shell script. This subshell reinitializes itself, so that the effect is as if a new shell had been invoked to interpret the script, with the exception that the locations of commands remembered by the parent (see the description of `hash` in Section 4.1 [Bourne Shell Builtins], page 42) are retained by the child.

Most versions of Unix make this a part of the operating system's command execution mechanism. If the first line of a script begins with the two characters '#!', the remainder of the line specifies an interpreter for the program. Thus, you can specify Bash, `awk`, Perl, or some other interpreter and write the rest of the script file in that language.

The arguments to the interpreter consist of a single optional argument following the interpreter name on the first line of the script file, followed by the name of the script file, followed by the rest of the arguments. Bash will perform this action on operating systems that do not handle it themselves. Note that some older versions of Unix limit the interpreter name and argument to a maximum of 32 characters.

Bash scripts often begin with `#! /bin/bash` (assuming that Bash has been installed in `/bin`), since this ensures that Bash will be used to interpret the script, even if it is executed under another shell.

4 Shell Builtin Commands

Builtin commands are contained within the shell itself. When the name of a builtin command is used as the first word of a simple command (see Section 3.2.1 [Simple Commands], page 8), the shell executes the command directly, without invoking another program. Builtin commands are necessary to implement functionality impossible or inconvenient to obtain with separate utilities.

This section briefly describes the builtins which Bash inherits from the Bourne Shell, as well as the builtin commands which are unique to or have been extended in Bash.

Several builtin commands are described in other chapters: builtin commands which provide the Bash interface to the job control facilities (see Section 7.2 [Job Control Builtins], page 101), the directory stack (see Section 6.8.1 [Directory Stack Builtins], page 93), the command history (see Section 9.2 [Bash History Builtins], page 137), and the programmable completion facilities (see Section 8.7 [Programmable Completion Builtins], page 131).

Many of the builtins have been extended by POSIX or Bash.

Unless otherwise noted, each builtin command documented as accepting options preceded by '-' accepts '--' to signify the end of the options. The :, `true`, `false`, and `test` builtins do not accept options and do not treat '--' specially. The `exit`, `logout`, `return`, `break`, `continue`, `let`, and `shift` builtins accept and process arguments beginning with '-' without requiring '--'. Other builtins that accept arguments but are not specified as accepting options interpret arguments beginning with '-' as invalid options and require '--' to prevent this interpretation.

4.1 Bourne Shell Builtins

The following shell builtin commands are inherited from the Bourne Shell. These commands are implemented as specified by the POSIX standard.

: (a colon)

> : [*arguments*]

> Do nothing beyond expanding *arguments* and performing redirections. The return status is zero.

. (a period)

> . *filename* [*arguments*]

> Read and execute commands from the *filename* argument in the current shell context. If *filename* does not contain a slash, the `PATH` variable is used to find *filename*. When Bash is not in POSIX mode, the current directory is searched if *filename* is not found in `$PATH`. If any *arguments* are supplied, they become the positional parameters when *filename* is executed. Otherwise the positional parameters are unchanged. If the `-T` option is enabled, `source` inherits any trap on `DEBUG`; if it is not, any `DEBUG` trap string is saved and restored around the call to `source`, and `source` unsets the `DEBUG` trap while it executes. If `-T` is not set, and the sourced file changes the `DEBUG` trap, the new value is retained when `source` completes. The return status is the exit status of the last command executed, or zero if no commands are executed. If *filename* is not found, or cannot be read, the return status is non-zero. This builtin is equivalent to `source`.

break

> ### break [*n*]
>
> Exit from a `for`, `while`, `until`, or `select` loop. If *n* is supplied, the *n*th enclosing loop is exited. *n* must be greater than or equal to 1. The return status is zero unless *n* is not greater than or equal to 1.

cd

> ### cd [-L|[-P [-e]]] [-@] [*directory*]
>
> Change the current working directory to *directory*. If *directory* is not supplied, the value of the `HOME` shell variable is used. Any additional arguments following *directory* are ignored. If the shell variable `CDPATH` exists, it is used as a search path: each directory name in `CDPATH` is searched for *directory*, with alternative directory names in `CDPATH` separated by a colon (':'). If *directory* begins with a slash, `CDPATH` is not used.
>
> The `-P` option means to not follow symbolic links: symbolic links are resolved while `cd` is traversing *directory* and before processing an instance of '..' in *directory*.
>
> By default, or when the `-L` option is supplied, symbolic links in *directory* are resolved after `cd` processes an instance of '..' in *directory*.
>
> If '..' appears in *directory*, it is processed by removing the immediately preceding pathname component, back to a slash or the beginning of *directory*.
>
> If the `-e` option is supplied with `-P` and the current working directory cannot be successfully determined after a successful directory change, `cd` will return an unsuccessful status.
>
> On systems that support it, the `-@` option presents the extended attributes associated with a file as a directory.
>
> If *directory* is '-', it is converted to `$OLDPWD` before the directory change is attempted.
>
> If a non-empty directory name from `CDPATH` is used, or if '-' is the first argument, and the directory change is successful, the absolute pathname of the new working directory is written to the standard output.
>
> The return status is zero if the directory is successfully changed, non-zero otherwise.

continue

> ### continue [*n*]
>
> Resume the next iteration of an enclosing `for`, `while`, `until`, or `select` loop. If *n* is supplied, the execution of the *n*th enclosing loop is resumed. *n* must be greater than or equal to 1. The return status is zero unless *n* is not greater than or equal to 1.

eval

> ### eval [*arguments*]
>
> The arguments are concatenated together into a single command, which is then read and executed, and its exit status returned as the exit status of `eval`. If there are no arguments or only empty arguments, the return status is zero.

exec

> exec [-cl] [-a *name*] [*command* [*arguments*]]

If *command* is supplied, it replaces the shell without creating a new process. If the -l option is supplied, the shell places a dash at the beginning of the zeroth argument passed to *command*. This is what the **login** program does. The -c option causes *command* to be executed with an empty environment. If -a is supplied, the shell passes *name* as the zeroth argument to *command*. If *command* cannot be executed for some reason, a non-interactive shell exits, unless the **execfail** shell option is enabled. In that case, it returns failure. An interactive shell returns failure if the file cannot be executed. If no *command* is specified, redirections may be used to affect the current shell environment. If there are no redirection errors, the return status is zero; otherwise the return status is non-zero.

exit

> exit [*n*]

Exit the shell, returning a status of *n* to the shell's parent. If *n* is omitted, the exit status is that of the last command executed. Any trap on **EXIT** is executed before the shell terminates.

export

> export [-fn] [-p] [*name*[=*value*]]

Mark each *name* to be passed to child processes in the environment. If the -f option is supplied, the *names* refer to shell functions; otherwise the names refer to shell variables. The -n option means to no longer mark each *name* for export. If no *names* are supplied, or if the -p option is given, a list of names of all exported variables is displayed. The -p option displays output in a form that may be reused as input. If a variable name is followed by =*value*, the value of the variable is set to *value*.

The return status is zero unless an invalid option is supplied, one of the names is not a valid shell variable name, or -f is supplied with a name that is not a shell function.

getopts

> getopts *optstring* *name* [*args*]

getopts is used by shell scripts to parse positional parameters. *optstring* contains the option characters to be recognized; if a character is followed by a colon, the option is expected to have an argument, which should be separated from it by whitespace. The colon (':') and question mark ('?') may not be used as option characters. Each time it is invoked, **getopts** places the next option in the shell variable *name*, initializing *name* if it does not exist, and the index of the next argument to be processed into the variable OPTIND. OPTIND is initialized to 1 each time the shell or a shell script is invoked. When an option requires an argument, **getopts** places that argument into the variable OPTARG. The shell does not reset OPTIND automatically; it must be manually reset between multiple calls to **getopts** within the same shell invocation if a new set of parameters is to be used.

When the end of options is encountered, `getopts` exits with a return value greater than zero. `OPTIND` is set to the index of the first non-option argument, and *name* is set to '?'.

`getopts` normally parses the positional parameters, but if more arguments are given in *args*, `getopts` parses those instead.

`getopts` can report errors in two ways. If the first character of *optstring* is a colon, *silent* error reporting is used. In normal operation, diagnostic messages are printed when invalid options or missing option arguments are encountered. If the variable `OPTERR` is set to 0, no error messages will be displayed, even if the first character of `optstring` is not a colon.

If an invalid option is seen, `getopts` places '?' into *name* and, if not silent, prints an error message and unsets `OPTARG`. If `getopts` is silent, the option character found is placed in `OPTARG` and no diagnostic message is printed.

If a required argument is not found, and `getopts` is not silent, a question mark ('?') is placed in *name*, `OPTARG` is unset, and a diagnostic message is printed. If `getopts` is silent, then a colon (':') is placed in *name* and `OPTARG` is set to the option character found.

hash

>   `hash [-r] [-p` *filename*`] [-dt] [`*name*`]`

Each time `hash` is invoked, it remembers the full pathnames of the commands specified as *name* arguments, so they need not be searched for on subsequent invocations. The commands are found by searching through the directories listed in `$PATH`. Any previously-remembered pathname is discarded. The `-p` option inhibits the path search, and *filename* is used as the location of *name*. The `-r` option causes the shell to forget all remembered locations. The `-d` option causes the shell to forget the remembered location of each *name*. If the `-t` option is supplied, the full pathname to which each *name* corresponds is printed. If multiple *name* arguments are supplied with `-t` the *name* is printed before the hashed full pathname. The `-l` option causes output to be displayed in a format that may be reused as input. If no arguments are given, or if only `-l` is supplied, information about remembered commands is printed. The return status is zero unless a *name* is not found or an invalid option is supplied.

pwd

>   `pwd [-LP]`

Print the absolute pathname of the current working directory. If the `-P` option is supplied, the pathname printed will not contain symbolic links. If the `-L` option is supplied, the pathname printed may contain symbolic links. The return status is zero unless an error is encountered while determining the name of the current directory or an invalid option is supplied.

readonly

>   `readonly [-aAf] [-p] [`*name*`[=`*value*`]] ...`

Mark each *name* as readonly. The values of these names may not be changed by subsequent assignment. If the `-f` option is supplied, each *name* refers to a shell function. The -a option means each *name* refers to an indexed array variable; the -A option means each *name* refers to an associative array variable. If both options are supplied, -A takes precedence. If no *name* arguments are given, or if the -p option is supplied, a list of all readonly names is printed. The other options may be used to restrict the output to a subset of the set of readonly names. The -p option causes output to be displayed in a format that may be reused as input. If a variable name is followed by =*value*, the value of the variable is set to *value*. The return status is zero unless an invalid option is supplied, one of the *name* arguments is not a valid shell variable or function name, or the -f option is supplied with a name that is not a shell function.

return

> **return** [*n*]
>
> Cause a shell function to stop executing and return the value *n* to its caller. If *n* is not supplied, the return value is the exit status of the last command executed in the function. If **return** is executed by a trap handler, the last command used to determine the status is the last command executed before the trap handler. if **return** is executed during a DEBUG trap, the last command used to determine the status is the last command executed by the trap handler before **return** was invoked. **return** may also be used to terminate execution of a script being executed with the . (**source**) builtin, returning either *n* or the exit status of the last command executed within the script as the exit status of the script. If *n* is supplied, the return value is its least significant 8 bits. Any command associated with the RETURN trap is executed before execution resumes after the function or script. The return status is non-zero if **return** is supplied a non-numeric argument or is used outside a function and not during the execution of a script by . or **source**.

shift

> **shift** [*n*]
>
> Shift the positional parameters to the left by *n*. The positional parameters from *n*+1 ... $# are renamed to $1 ... $#-*n*. Parameters represented by the numbers $# to $#-*n*+1 are unset. *n* must be a non-negative number less than or equal to $#. If *n* is zero or greater than $#, the positional parameters are not changed. If *n* is not supplied, it is assumed to be 1. The return status is zero unless *n* is greater than $# or less than zero, non-zero otherwise.

test
[

> **test** *expr*
>
> Evaluate a conditional expression *expr* and return a status of 0 (true) or 1 (false). Each operator and operand must be a separate argument. Expressions are composed of the primaries described below in Section 6.4 [Bash Conditional Expressions], page 87. **test** does not accept any options, nor does it accept and ignore an argument of -- as signifying the end of options.
>
> When the [form is used, the last argument to the command must be a].

Expressions may be combined using the following operators, listed in decreasing order of precedence. The evaluation depends on the number of arguments; see below. Operator precedence is used when there are five or more arguments.

`! expr`   True if *expr* is false.

`( expr )`   Returns the value of *expr*. This may be used to override the normal precedence of operators.

`expr1 -a expr2`
> True if both *expr1* and *expr2* are true.

`expr1 -o expr2`
> True if either *expr1* or *expr2* is true.

The `test` and `[` builtins evaluate conditional expressions using a set of rules based on the number of arguments.

0 arguments
> The expression is false.

1 argument
> The expression is true if and only if the argument is not null.

2 arguments
> If the first argument is '`!`', the expression is true if and only if the second argument is null. If the first argument is one of the unary conditional operators (see Section 6.4 [Bash Conditional Expressions], page 87), the expression is true if the unary test is true. If the first argument is not a valid unary operator, the expression is false.

3 arguments
> The following conditions are applied in the order listed. If the second argument is one of the binary conditional operators (see Section 6.4 [Bash Conditional Expressions], page 87), the result of the expression is the result of the binary test using the first and third arguments as operands. The '`-a`' and '`-o`' operators are considered binary operators when there are three arguments. If the first argument is '`!`', the value is the negation of the two-argument test using the second and third arguments. If the first argument is exactly '`(`' and the third argument is exactly '`)`', the result is the one-argument test of the second argument. Otherwise, the expression is false.

4 arguments
> If the first argument is '`!`', the result is the negation of the three-argument expression composed of the remaining arguments. Otherwise, the expression is parsed and evaluated according to precedence using the rules listed above.

5 or more arguments
> The expression is parsed and evaluated according to precedence using the rules listed above.

When used with `test` or '[', the '<' and '>' operators sort lexicographically using ASCII ordering.

times

> `times`

Print out the user and system times used by the shell and its children. The return status is zero.

trap

> `trap [-lp] [arg] [sigspec ...]`

The commands in *arg* are to be read and executed when the shell receives signal *sigspec*. If *arg* is absent (and there is a single *sigspec*) or equal to '-', each specified signal's disposition is reset to the value it had when the shell was started. If *arg* is the null string, then the signal specified by each *sigspec* is ignored by the shell and commands it invokes. If *arg* is not present and -p has been supplied, the shell displays the trap commands associated with each *sigspec*. If no arguments are supplied, or only -p is given, `trap` prints the list of commands associated with each signal number in a form that may be reused as shell input. The -l option causes the shell to print a list of signal names and their corresponding numbers. Each *sigspec* is either a signal name or a signal number. Signal names are case insensitive and the `SIG` prefix is optional.

If a *sigspec* is 0 or EXIT, *arg* is executed when the shell exits. If a *sigspec* is DEBUG, the command *arg* is executed before every simple command, `for` command, `case` command, `select` command, every arithmetic `for` command, and before the first command executes in a shell function. Refer to the description of the `extdebug` option to the `shopt` builtin (see Section 4.3.2 [The Shopt Builtin], page 64) for details of its effect on the DEBUG trap. If a *sigspec* is RETURN, the command *arg* is executed each time a shell function or a script executed with the . or `source` builtins finishes executing.

If a *sigspec* is ERR, the command *arg* is executed whenever a pipeline (which may consist of a single simple command), a list, or a compound command returns a non-zero exit status, subject to the following conditions. The ERR trap is not executed if the failed command is part of the command list immediately following an `until` or `while` keyword, part of the test following the `if` or `elif` reserved words, part of a command executed in a `&&` or `||` list except the command following the final `&&` or `||`, any command in a pipeline but the last, or if the command's return status is being inverted using !. These are the same conditions obeyed by the `errexit` (-e) option.

Signals ignored upon entry to the shell cannot be trapped or reset. Trapped signals that are not being ignored are reset to their original values in a subshell or subshell environment when one is created.

The return status is zero unless a *sigspec* does not specify a valid signal.

umask

> `umask [-p] [-S] [mode]`

Set the shell process's file creation mask to *mode*. If *mode* begins with a digit, it is interpreted as an octal number; if not, it is interpreted as a symbolic mode mask similar to that accepted by the `chmod` command. If *mode* is omitted, the current value of the mask is printed. If the `-S` option is supplied without a *mode* argument, the mask is printed in a symbolic format. If the `-p` option is supplied, and *mode* is omitted, the output is in a form that may be reused as input. The return status is zero if the mode is successfully changed or if no *mode* argument is supplied, and non-zero otherwise.

Note that when the mode is interpreted as an octal number, each number of the umask is subtracted from 7. Thus, a umask of 022 results in permissions of 755.

`unset`

> `unset [-fnv] [name]`

> Remove each variable or function *name*. If the `-v` option is given, each *name* refers to a shell variable and that variable is removed. If the `-f` option is given, the *name*s refer to shell functions, and the function definition is removed. If the `-n` option is supplied, and *name* is a variable with the *nameref* attribute, *name* will be unset rather than the variable it references. `-n` has no effect if the `-f` option is supplied. If no options are supplied, each *name* refers to a variable; if there is no variable by that name, any function with that name is unset. Readonly variables and functions may not be unset. The return status is zero unless a *name* is readonly.

4.2 Bash Builtin Commands

This section describes builtin commands which are unique to or have been extended in Bash. Some of these commands are specified in the POSIX standard.

`alias`

> `alias [-p] [name[=value] ...]`

> Without arguments or with the `-p` option, `alias` prints the list of aliases on the standard output in a form that allows them to be reused as input. If arguments are supplied, an alias is defined for each *name* whose *value* is given. If no *value* is given, the name and value of the alias is printed. Aliases are described in Section 6.6 [Aliases], page 90.

`bind`

> ```
> bind [-m keymap] [-lpsvPSVX]
> bind [-m keymap] [-q function] [-u function] [-r keyseq]
> bind [-m keymap] -f filename
> bind [-m keymap] -x keyseq:shell-command
> bind [-m keymap] keyseq:function-name
> bind [-m keymap] keyseq:readline-command
> ```

> Display current Readline (see Chapter 8 [Command Line Editing], page 104) key and function bindings, bind a key sequence to a Readline function or macro, or set a Readline variable. Each non-option argument is a command as it would appear in a Readline initialization file (see Section 8.3 [Readline Init File], page 107), but each binding or command must be passed as a separate argument; e.g., '`"\C-x\C-r":re-read-init-file`'.

Options, if supplied, have the following meanings:

-m *keymap*   Use *keymap* as the keymap to be affected by the subsequent bindings. Acceptable *keymap* names are `emacs`, `emacs-standard`, `emacs-meta`, `emacs-ctlx`, `vi`, `vi-move`, `vi-command`, and `vi-insert`. `vi` is equivalent to `vi-command` (`vi-move` is also a synonym); `emacs` is equivalent to `emacs-standard`.

-l   List the names of all Readline functions.

-p   Display Readline function names and bindings in such a way that they can be used as input or in a Readline initialization file.

-P   List current Readline function names and bindings.

-v   Display Readline variable names and values in such a way that they can be used as input or in a Readline initialization file.

-V   List current Readline variable names and values.

-s   Display Readline key sequences bound to macros and the strings they output in such a way that they can be used as input or in a Readline initialization file.

-S   Display Readline key sequences bound to macros and the strings they output.

-f *filename*
              Read key bindings from *filename*.

-q *function*
              Query about which keys invoke the named *function*.

-u *function*
              Unbind all keys bound to the named *function*.

-r *keyseq*   Remove any current binding for *keyseq*.

-x *keyseq:shell-command*
              Cause *shell-command* to be executed whenever *keyseq* is entered. When *shell-command* is executed, the shell sets the `READLINE_LINE` variable to the contents of the Readline line buffer and the `READLINE_POINT` variable to the current location of the insertion point. If the executed command changes the value of `READLINE_LINE` or `READLINE_POINT`, those new values will be reflected in the editing state.

-X   List all key sequences bound to shell commands and the associated commands in a format that can be reused as input.

The return status is zero unless an invalid option is supplied or an error occurs.

`builtin`

          `builtin [`*shell-builtin* `[`*args*`]]`
Run a shell builtin, passing it *args*, and return its exit status. This is useful when defining a shell function with the same name as a shell builtin, retaining

the functionality of the builtin within the function. The return status is non-zero if *shell-builtin* is not a shell builtin command.

`caller`

`caller [`*expr*`]`

Returns the context of any active subroutine call (a shell function or a script executed with the . or `source` builtins).

Without *expr*, `caller` displays the line number and source filename of the current subroutine call. If a non-negative integer is supplied as *expr*, `caller` displays the line number, subroutine name, and source file corresponding to that position in the current execution call stack. This extra information may be used, for example, to print a stack trace. The current frame is frame 0.

The return value is 0 unless the shell is not executing a subroutine call or *expr* does not correspond to a valid position in the call stack.

`command`

`command [-pVv]` *command* `[`*arguments* `...]`

Runs *command* with *arguments* ignoring any shell function named *command*. Only shell builtin commands or commands found by searching the PATH are executed. If there is a shell function named `ls`, running 'command ls' within the function will execute the external command `ls` instead of calling the function recursively. The -p option means to use a default value for PATH that is guaranteed to find all of the standard utilities. The return status in this case is 127 if *command* cannot be found or an error occurred, and the exit status of *command* otherwise.

If either the -V or -v option is supplied, a description of *command* is printed. The -v option causes a single word indicating the command or file name used to invoke *command* to be displayed; the -V option produces a more verbose description. In this case, the return status is zero if *command* is found, and non-zero if not.

`declare`

`declare [-aAfFgilnrtux] [-p] [`*name*`[=`*value*`] ...]`

Declare variables and give them attributes. If no *names* are given, then display the values of variables instead.

The -p option will display the attributes and values of each *name*. When -p is used with *name* arguments, additional options, other than -f and -F, are ignored.

When -p is supplied without *name* arguments, `declare` will display the attributes and values of all variables having the attributes specified by the additional options. If no other options are supplied with -p, `declare` will display the attributes and values of all shell variables. The -f option will restrict the display to shell functions.

The -F option inhibits the display of function definitions; only the function name and attributes are printed. If the `extdebug` shell option is enabled using `shopt` (see Section 4.3.2 [The Shopt Builtin], page 64), the source file name and line number where each *name* is defined are displayed as well. `-F` implies `-f`.

The `-g` option forces variables to be created or modified at the global scope, even when `declare` is executed in a shell function. It is ignored in all other cases.

The following options can be used to restrict output to variables with the specified attributes or to give variables attributes:

`-a`   Each *name* is an indexed array variable (see Section 6.7 [Arrays], page 91).

`-A`   Each *name* is an associative array variable (see Section 6.7 [Arrays], page 91).

`-f`   Use function names only.

`-i`   The variable is to be treated as an integer; arithmetic evaluation (see Section 6.5 [Shell Arithmetic], page 89) is performed when the variable is assigned a value.

`-l`   When the variable is assigned a value, all upper-case characters are converted to lower-case. The upper-case attribute is disabled.

`-n`   Give each *name* the *nameref* attribute, making it a name reference to another variable. That other variable is defined by the value of *name*. All references, assignments, and attribute modifications to *name*, except for those using or changing the `-n` attribute itself, are performed on the variable referenced by *name*'s value. The nameref attribute cannot be applied to array variables.

`-r`   Make *names* readonly. These names cannot then be assigned values by subsequent assignment statements or unset.

`-t`   Give each *name* the `trace` attribute. Traced functions inherit the `DEBUG` and `RETURN` traps from the calling shell. The trace attribute has no special meaning for variables.

`-u`   When the variable is assigned a value, all lower-case characters are converted to upper-case. The lower-case attribute is disabled.

`-x`   Mark each *name* for export to subsequent commands via the environment.

Using '+' instead of '−' turns off the attribute instead, with the exceptions that '+a' may not be used to destroy an array variable and '+r' will not remove the readonly attribute. When used in a function, `declare` makes each *name* local, as with the `local` command, unless the `-g` option is used. If a variable name is followed by =*value*, the value of the variable is set to *value*.

When using `-a` or `-A` and the compound assignment syntax to create array variables, additional attributes do not take effect until subsequent assignments.

The return status is zero unless an invalid option is encountered, an attempt is made to define a function using '`-f foo=bar`', an attempt is made to assign a value to a readonly variable, an attempt is made to assign a value to an array variable without using the compound assignment syntax (see Section 6.7 [Arrays], page 91), one of the *names* is not a valid shell variable name, an attempt is made to turn off readonly status for a readonly variable, an attempt is made to turn off array status for an array variable, or an attempt is made to display a non-existent function with `-f`.

echo

> echo [-neE] [*arg* ...]

Output the *args*, separated by spaces, terminated with a newline. The return status is 0 unless a write error occurs. If `-n` is specified, the trailing newline is suppressed. If the `-e` option is given, interpretation of the following backslash-escaped characters is enabled. The `-E` option disables the interpretation of these escape characters, even on systems where they are interpreted by default. The `xpg_echo` shell option may be used to dynamically determine whether or not `echo` expands these escape characters by default. `echo` does not interpret `--` to mean the end of options.

echo interprets the following escape sequences:

`\a`   alert (bell)

`\b`   backspace

`\c`   suppress further output

`\e`
`\E`   escape

`\f`   form feed

`\n`   new line

`\r`   carriage return

`\t`   horizontal tab

`\v`   vertical tab

`\\`   backslash

`\0`*nnn*   the eight-bit character whose value is the octal value *nnn* (zero to three octal digits)

`\x`*HH*   the eight-bit character whose value is the hexadecimal value *HH* (one or two hex digits)

`\u`*HHHH*   the Unicode (ISO/IEC 10646) character whose value is the hexadecimal value *HHHH* (one to four hex digits)

`\U`*HHHHHHHH*
          the Unicode (ISO/IEC 10646) character whose value is the hexadecimal value *HHHHHHHH* (one to eight hex digits)

enable

> enable [-a] [-dnps] [-f *filename*] [*name* ...]

Enable and disable builtin shell commands. Disabling a builtin allows a disk command which has the same name as a shell builtin to be executed without specifying a full pathname, even though the shell normally searches for builtins before disk commands. If -n is used, the *names* become disabled. Otherwise *names* are enabled. For example, to use the `test` binary found via `$PATH` instead of the shell builtin version, type 'enable -n test'.

If the -p option is supplied, or no *name* arguments appear, a list of shell builtins is printed. With no other arguments, the list consists of all enabled shell builtins. The -a option means to list each builtin with an indication of whether or not it is enabled.

The -f option means to load the new builtin command *name* from shared object *filename*, on systems that support dynamic loading. The -d option will delete a builtin loaded with -f.

If there are no options, a list of the shell builtins is displayed. The -s option restricts `enable` to the POSIX special builtins. If -s is used with -f, the new builtin becomes a special builtin (see Section 4.4 [Special Builtins], page 70).

The return status is zero unless a *name* is not a shell builtin or there is an error loading a new builtin from a shared object.

help

      `help [-dms] [`*`pattern`*`]`

Display helpful information about builtin commands. If *pattern* is specified, `help` gives detailed help on all commands matching *pattern*, otherwise a list of the builtins is printed.

Options, if supplied, have the following meanings:

-d   Display a short description of each *pattern*

-m   Display the description of each *pattern* in a manpage-like format

-s   Display only a short usage synopsis for each *pattern*

The return status is zero unless no command matches *pattern*.

let

      `let `*`expression`*` [`*`expression`*` ...]`

The `let` builtin allows arithmetic to be performed on shell variables. Each *expression* is evaluated according to the rules given below in Section 6.5 [Shell Arithmetic], page 89. If the last *expression* evaluates to 0, `let` returns 1; otherwise 0 is returned.

local

      `local [`*`option`*`] `*`name`*`[=`*`value`*`] ...`

For each argument, a local variable named *name* is created, and assigned *value*. The *option* can be any of the options accepted by `declare`. `local` can only be used within a function; it makes the variable *name* have a visible scope restricted to that function and its children. If *name* is '-', the set of shell options is made local to the function in which `local` is invoked: shell options changed using the `set` builtin inside the function are restored to their original values when the function returns. The return status is zero unless `local` is used outside a function, an invalid *name* is supplied, or *name* is a readonly variable.

logout

>   `logout [n]`
>
> Exit a login shell, returning a status of *n* to the shell's parent.

mapfile

>   `mapfile [-d delim] [-n count] [-O origin] [-s count] [-t] [-u fd]`
>   `[-C callback] [-c quantum] [array]`
>
> Read lines from the standard input into the indexed array variable *array*, or from file descriptor *fd* if the `-u` option is supplied. The variable `MAPFILE` is the default *array*. Options, if supplied, have the following meanings:

-d
: The first character of *delim* is used to terminate each input line, rather than newline.

-n
: Copy at most *count* lines. If *count* is 0, all lines are copied.

-O
: Begin assigning to *array* at index *origin*. The default index is 0.

-s
: Discard the first *count* lines read.

-t
: Remove a trailing *delim* (default newline) from each line read.

-u
: Read lines from file descriptor *fd* instead of the standard input.

-C
: Evaluate *callback* each time *quantum*P lines are read. The `-c` option specifies *quantum*.

-c
: Specify the number of lines read between each call to *callback*.

> If `-C` is specified without `-c`, the default quantum is 5000. When *callback* is evaluated, it is supplied the index of the next array element to be assigned and the line to be assigned to that element as additional arguments. *callback* is evaluated after the line is read but before the array element is assigned.
>
> If not supplied with an explicit origin, `mapfile` will clear *array* before assigning to it.
>
> `mapfile` returns successfully unless an invalid option or option argument is supplied, *array* is invalid or unassignable, or *array* is not an indexed array.

printf

>   `printf [-v var] format [arguments]`
>
> Write the formatted *arguments* to the standard output under the control of the *format*. The `-v` option causes the output to be assigned to the variable *var* rather than being printed to the standard output.
>
> The *format* is a character string which contains three types of objects: plain characters, which are simply copied to standard output, character escape sequences, which are converted and copied to the standard output, and format specifications, each of which causes printing of the next successive *argument*.

In addition to the standard `printf(1)` formats, `printf` interprets the following extensions:

`%b`   Causes `printf` to expand backslash escape sequences in the corresponding *argument* in the same way as `echo -e` (see Section 4.2 [Bash Builtins], page 49).

`%q`   Causes `printf` to output the corresponding *argument* in a format that can be reused as shell input.

`%(datefmt)T`

Causes `printf` to output the date-time string resulting from using *datefmt* as a format string for `strftime(3)`. The corresponding *argument* is an integer representing the number of seconds since the epoch. Two special argument values may be used: -1 represents the current time, and -2 represents the time the shell was invoked. If no argument is specified, conversion behaves as if -1 had been given. This is an exception to the usual `printf` behavior.

Arguments to non-string format specifiers are treated as C language constants, except that a leading plus or minus sign is allowed, and if the leading character is a single or double quote, the value is the ASCII value of the following character.

The *format* is reused as necessary to consume all of the *arguments*. If the *format* requires more *arguments* than are supplied, the extra format specifications behave as if a zero value or null string, as appropriate, had been supplied. The return value is zero on success, non-zero on failure.

`read`

```
read [-ers] [-a aname] [-d delim] [-i text] [-n nchars]
     [-N nchars] [-p prompt] [-t timeout] [-u fd] [name ...]
```

One line is read from the standard input, or from the file descriptor *fd* supplied as an argument to the `-u` option, split into words as described above in Section 3.5.7 [Word Splitting], page 30, and the first word is assigned to the first *name*, the second word to the second *name*, and so on. If there are more words than names, the remaining words and their intervening delimiters are assigned to the last *name*. If there are fewer words read from the input stream than names, the remaining names are assigned empty values. The characters in the value of the `IFS` variable are used to split the line into words using the same rules the shell uses for expansion (described above in Section 3.5.7 [Word Splitting], page 30). The backslash character '\' may be used to remove any special meaning for the next character read and for line continuation. If no names are supplied, the line read is assigned to the variable `REPLY`. The exit status is zero, unless end-of-file is encountered, `read` times out (in which case the status is greater than 128), a variable assignment error (such as assigning to a readonly variable) occurs, or an invalid file descriptor is supplied as the argument to `-u`.

Options, if supplied, have the following meanings:

-a *aname*   The words are assigned to sequential indices of the array variable *aname*, starting at 0. All elements are removed from *aname* before the assignment. Other *name* arguments are ignored.

-d *delim*   The first character of *delim* is used to terminate the input line, rather than newline.

-e   Readline (see Chapter 8 [Command Line Editing], page 104) is used to obtain the line. Readline uses the current (or default, if line editing was not previously active) editing settings.

-i *text*   If Readline is being used to read the line, *text* is placed into the editing buffer before editing begins.

-n *nchars*   **read** returns after reading *nchars* characters rather than waiting for a complete line of input, but honors a delimiter if fewer than *nchars* characters are read before the delimiter.

-N *nchars*   **read** returns after reading exactly *nchars* characters rather than waiting for a complete line of input, unless EOF is encountered or **read** times out. Delimiter characters encountered in the input are not treated specially and do not cause **read** to return until *nchars* characters are read. The result is not split on the characters in IFS; the intent is that the variable is assigned exactly the characters read (with the exception of backslash; see the -**r** option below).

-p *prompt*   Display *prompt*, without a trailing newline, before attempting to read any input. The prompt is displayed only if input is coming from a terminal.

-r   If this option is given, backslash does not act as an escape character. The backslash is considered to be part of the line. In particular, a backslash-newline pair may not be used as a line continuation.

-s   Silent mode. If input is coming from a terminal, characters are not echoed.

-t *timeout*

    Cause **read** to time out and return failure if a complete line of input (or a specified number of characters) is not read within *timeout* seconds. *timeout* may be a decimal number with a fractional portion following the decimal point. This option is only effective if **read** is reading input from a terminal, pipe, or other special file; it has no effect when reading from regular files. If **read** times out, **read** saves any partial input read into the specified variable *name*. If *timeout* is 0, **read** returns immediately, without trying to read and data. The exit status is 0 if input is available on the specified file descriptor, non-zero otherwise. The exit status is greater than 128 if the timeout is exceeded.

-u *fd*   Read input from file descriptor *fd*.

readarray

        readarray [-d *delim*] [-n *count*] [-O *origin*] [-s *count*] [-t] [-u *fd*]

                 `[-C callback] [-c quantum] [array]`

Read lines from the standard input into the indexed array variable *array*, or from file descriptor *fd* if the `-u` option is supplied.

A synonym for `mapfile`.

`source`

         `source filename`

A synonym for . (see Section 4.1 [Bourne Shell Builtins], page 42).

`type`

         `type [-afptP] [name ...]`

For each *name*, indicate how it would be interpreted if used as a command name.

If the `-t` option is used, `type` prints a single word which is one of 'alias', 'function', 'builtin', 'file' or 'keyword', if *name* is an alias, shell function, shell builtin, disk file, or shell reserved word, respectively. If the *name* is not found, then nothing is printed, and `type` returns a failure status.

If the `-p` option is used, `type` either returns the name of the disk file that would be executed, or nothing if `-t` would not return 'file'.

The `-P` option forces a path search for each *name*, even if `-t` would not return 'file'.

If a command is hashed, `-p` and `-P` print the hashed value, which is not necessarily the file that appears first in `$PATH`.

If the `-a` option is used, `type` returns all of the places that contain an executable named *file*. This includes aliases and functions, if and only if the `-p` option is not also used.

If the `-f` option is used, `type` does not attempt to find shell functions, as with the `command` builtin.

The return status is zero if all of the *names* are found, non-zero if any are not found.

`typeset`

         `typeset [-afFgrxilnrtux] [-p] [name[=value] ...]`

The `typeset` command is supplied for compatibility with the Korn shell. It is a synonym for the `declare` builtin command.

`ulimit`

         `ulimit [-HSabcdefiklmnpqrstuvxPT] [limit]`

`ulimit` provides control over the resources available to processes started by the shell, on systems that allow such control. If an option is given, it is interpreted as follows:

`-S`   Change and report the soft limit associated with a resource.

`-H`   Change and report the hard limit associated with a resource.

`-a`   All current limits are reported.

-b	The maximum socket buffer size.
-c	The maximum size of core files created.
-d	The maximum size of a process's data segment.
-e	The maximum scheduling priority ("nice").
-f	The maximum size of files written by the shell and its children.
-i	The maximum number of pending signals.
-k	The maximum number of kqueues that may be allocated.
-l	The maximum size that may be locked into memory.
-m	The maximum resident set size (many systems do not honor this limit).
-n	The maximum number of open file descriptors (most systems do not allow this value to be set).
-p	The pipe buffer size.
-q	The maximum number of bytes in POSIX message queues.
-r	The maximum real-time scheduling priority.
-s	The maximum stack size.
-t	The maximum amount of cpu time in seconds.
-u	The maximum number of processes available to a single user.
-v	The maximum amount of virtual memory available to the shell, and, on some systems, to its children.
-x	The maximum number of file locks.
-P	The maximum number of pseudoterminals.
-T	The maximum number of threads.

If *limit* is given, and the -a option is not used, *limit* is the new value of the specified resource. The special *limit* values `hard`, `soft`, and `unlimited` stand for the current hard limit, the current soft limit, and no limit, respectively. A hard limit cannot be increased by a non-root user once it is set; a soft limit may be increased up to the value of the hard limit. Otherwise, the current value of the soft limit for the specified resource is printed, unless the -H option is supplied. When setting new limits, if neither -H nor -S is supplied, both the hard and soft limits are set. If no option is given, then -f is assumed. Values are in 1024-byte increments, except for -t, which is in seconds; -p, which is in units of 512-byte blocks; -P, -T, -b, -k, -n and -u, which are unscaled values; and, when in POSIX Mode (see Section 6.11 [Bash POSIX Mode], page 96), -c and -f, which are in 512-byte increments.

The return status is zero unless an invalid option or argument is supplied, or an error occurs while setting a new limit.

unalias

> unalias [-a] [*name* ...]

> Remove each *name* from the list of aliases. If -a is supplied, all aliases are removed. Aliases are described in Section 6.6 [Aliases], page 90.

4.3 Modifying Shell Behavior

4.3.1 The Set Builtin

This builtin is so complicated that it deserves its own section. set allows you to change the values of shell options and set the positional parameters, or to display the names and values of shell variables.

set

> set [--abefhkmnptuvxBCEHPT] [-o *option-name*] [*argument* ...]
> set [+abefhkmnptuvxBCEHPT] [+o *option-name*] [*argument* ...]

If no options or arguments are supplied, set displays the names and values of all shell variables and functions, sorted according to the current locale, in a format that may be reused as input for setting or resetting the currently-set variables. Read-only variables cannot be reset. In POSIX mode, only shell variables are listed.

When options are supplied, they set or unset shell attributes. Options, if specified, have the following meanings:

-a
: Each variable or function that is created or modified is given the export attribute and marked for export to the environment of subsequent commands.

-b
: Cause the status of terminated background jobs to be reported immediately, rather than before printing the next primary prompt.

-e
: Exit immediately if a pipeline (see Section 3.2.2 [Pipelines], page 8), which may consist of a single simple command (see Section 3.2.1 [Simple Commands], page 8), a list (see Section 3.2.3 [Lists], page 9), or a compound command (see Section 3.2.4 [Compound Commands], page 9) returns a non-zero status. The shell does not exit if the command that fails is part of the command list immediately following a while or until keyword, part of the test in an if statement, part of any command executed in a && or || list except the command following the final && or ||, any command in a pipeline but the last, or if the command's return status is being inverted with !. If a compound command other than a subshell returns a non-zero status because a command failed while -e was being ignored, the shell does not exit. A trap on ERR, if set, is executed before the shell exits.

: This option applies to the shell environment and each subshell environment separately (see Section 3.7.3 [Command Execution Environment], page 37), and may cause subshells to exit before executing all the commands in the subshell.

If a compound command or shell function executes in a context where -e is being ignored, none of the commands executed within the compound command or function body will be affected by the -e setting, even if -e is set and a command returns a failure status. If a compound command or shell function sets -e while executing in a context where -e is ignored, that setting will not have any effect until the compound command or the command containing the function call completes.

-f   Disable filename expansion (globbing).

-h   Locate and remember (hash) commands as they are looked up for execution. This option is enabled by default.

-k   All arguments in the form of assignment statements are placed in the environment for a command, not just those that precede the command name.

-m   Job control is enabled (see Chapter 7 [Job Control], page 100). All processes run in a separate process group. When a background job completes, the shell prints a line containing its exit status.

-n   Read commands but do not execute them. This may be used to check a script for syntax errors. This option is ignored by interactive shells.

-o *option-name*

Set the option corresponding to *option-name*:

allexport
> Same as -a.

braceexpand
> Same as -B.

emacs   Use an **emacs**-style line editing interface (see Chapter 8 [Command Line Editing], page 104). This also affects the editing interface used for **read -e**.

errexit   Same as -e.

errtrace   Same as -E.

functrace
> Same as -T.

hashall   Same as -h.

histexpand
> Same as -H.

history   Enable command history, as described in Section 9.1 [Bash History Facilities], page 137. This option is on by default in interactive shells.

ignoreeof
> An interactive shell will not exit upon reading EOF.

keyword Same as -k.

monitor Same as -m.

noclobber

Same as -C.

noexec   Same as -n.

noglob   Same as -f.

nolog   Currently ignored.

notify   Same as -b.

nounset Same as -u.

onecmd   Same as -t.

physical Same as -P.

pipefail If set, the return value of a pipeline is the value of
the last (rightmost) command to exit with a non-zero
status, or zero if all commands in the pipeline exit successfully. This option is disabled by default.

posix   Change the behavior of Bash where the default operation differs from the POSIX standard to match the standard (see Section 6.11 [Bash POSIX Mode], page 96).
This is intended to make Bash behave as a strict superset of that standard.

privileged

Same as -p.

verbose Same as -v.

vi   Use a vi-style line editing interface. This also affects
the editing interface used for read -e.

xtrace   Same as -x.

-p   Turn on privileged mode. In this mode, the $BASH_ENV and $ENV
files are not processed, shell functions are not inherited from the environment, and the SHELLOPTS, BASHOPTS, CDPATH and GLOBIGNORE
variables, if they appear in the environment, are ignored. If the shell
is started with the effective user (group) id not equal to the real
user (group) id, and the -p option is not supplied, these actions
are taken and the effective user id is set to the real user id. If the
-p option is supplied at startup, the effective user id is not reset.
Turning this option off causes the effective user and group ids to
be set to the real user and group ids.

-t   Exit after reading and executing one command.

-u   Treat unset variables and parameters other than the special parameters '@' or '*' as an error when performing parameter expansion.

An error message will be written to the standard error, and a non-interactive shell will exit.

`-v`   Print shell input lines as they are read.

`-x`   Print a trace of simple commands, `for` commands, `case` commands, `select` commands, and arithmetic `for` commands and their arguments or associated word lists after they are expanded and before they are executed. The value of the `PS4` variable is expanded and the resultant value is printed before the command and its expanded arguments.

`-B`   The shell will perform brace expansion (see Section 3.5.1 [Brace Expansion], page 21). This option is on by default.

`-C`   Prevent output redirection using '>', '>&', and '<>' from overwriting existing files.

`-E`   If set, any trap on `ERR` is inherited by shell functions, command substitutions, and commands executed in a subshell environment. The `ERR` trap is normally not inherited in such cases.

`-H`   Enable '!' style history substitution (see Section 9.3 [History Interaction], page 139). This option is on by default for interactive shells.

`-P`   If set, do not resolve symbolic links when performing commands such as `cd` which change the current directory. The physical directory is used instead. By default, Bash follows the logical chain of directories when performing commands which change the current directory.

For example, if `/usr/sys` is a symbolic link to `/usr/local/sys` then:

```
$ cd /usr/sys; echo $PWD
/usr/sys
$ cd ..; pwd
/usr
```

If `set -P` is on, then:

```
$ cd /usr/sys; echo $PWD
/usr/local/sys
$ cd ..; pwd
/usr/local
```

`-T`   If set, any trap on `DEBUG` and `RETURN` are inherited by shell functions, command substitutions, and commands executed in a subshell environment. The `DEBUG` and `RETURN` traps are normally not inherited in such cases.

`--`   If no arguments follow this option, then the positional parameters are unset. Otherwise, the positional parameters are set to the *arguments*, even if some of them begin with a '-'.

- Signal the end of options, cause all remaining *arguments* to be assigned to the positional parameters. The -x and -v options are turned off. If there are no arguments, the positional parameters remain unchanged.

Using '+' rather than '-' causes these options to be turned off. The options can also be used upon invocation of the shell. The current set of options may be found in $-.

The remaining N *arguments* are positional parameters and are assigned, in order, to $1, $2, ... $N. The special parameter # is set to N.

The return status is always zero unless an invalid option is supplied.

4.3.2 The Shopt Builtin

This builtin allows you to change additional shell optional behavior.

shopt

shopt [-pqsu] [-o] [*optname* ...]

Toggle the values of settings controlling optional shell behavior. The settings can be either those listed below, or, if the -o option is used, those available with the -o option to the set builtin command (see Section 4.3.1 [The Set Builtin], page 60). With no options, or with the -p option, a list of all settable options is displayed, with an indication of whether or not each is set. The -p option causes output to be displayed in a form that may be reused as input. Other options have the following meanings:

-s   Enable (set) each *optname*.

-u   Disable (unset) each *optname*.

-q   Suppresses normal output; the return status indicates whether the *optname* is set or unset. If multiple *optname* arguments are given with -q, the return status is zero if all *optnames* are enabled; non-zero otherwise.

-o   Restricts the values of *optname* to be those defined for the -o option to the set builtin (see Section 4.3.1 [The Set Builtin], page 60).

If either -s or -u is used with no *optname* arguments, shopt shows only those options which are set or unset, respectively.

Unless otherwise noted, the shopt options are disabled (off) by default.

The return status when listing options is zero if all *optnames* are enabled, non-zero otherwise. When setting or unsetting options, the return status is zero unless an *optname* is not a valid shell option.

The list of shopt options is:

autocd   If set, a command name that is the name of a directory is executed as if it were the argument to the cd command. This option is only used by interactive shells.

cdable_vars
> If this is set, an argument to the `cd` builtin command that is not a directory is assumed to be the name of a variable whose value is the directory to change to.

cdspell
> If set, minor errors in the spelling of a directory component in a `cd` command will be corrected. The errors checked for are transposed characters, a missing character, and a character too many. If a correction is found, the corrected path is printed, and the command proceeds. This option is only used by interactive shells.

checkhash
> If this is set, Bash checks that a command found in the hash table exists before trying to execute it. If a hashed command no longer exists, a normal path search is performed.

checkjobs
> If set, Bash lists the status of any stopped and running jobs before exiting an interactive shell. If any jobs are running, this causes the exit to be deferred until a second exit is attempted without an intervening command (see Chapter 7 [Job Control], page 100). The shell always postpones exiting if any jobs are stopped.

checkwinsize
> If set, Bash checks the window size after each command and, if necessary, updates the values of LINES and COLUMNS.

cmdhist
> If set, Bash attempts to save all lines of a multiple-line command in the same history entry. This allows easy re-editing of multi-line commands.

compat31
> If set, Bash changes its behavior to that of version 3.1 with respect to quoted arguments to the conditional command's '=~' operator and with respect to locale-specific string comparison when using the [[conditional command's '<' and '>' operators. Bash versions prior to bash-4.1 use ASCII collation and strcmp(3); bash-4.1 and later use the current locale's collation sequence and strcoll(3).

compat32
> If set, Bash changes its behavior to that of version 3.2 with respect to locale-specific string comparison when using the [[conditional command's '<' and '>' operators (see previous item) and the effect of interrupting a command list. Bash versions 3.2 and earlier continue with the next command in the list after one terminates due to an interrupt.

compat40
> If set, Bash changes its behavior to that of version 4.0 with respect to locale-specific string comparison when using the [[conditional command's '<' and '>' operators (see description of compat31) and the effect of interrupting a command list. Bash versions 4.0 and later interrupt the list as if the shell received the interrupt; previous versions continue with the next command in the list.

compat41   If set, Bash, when in POSIX mode, treats a single quote in a double-quoted parameter expansion as a special character. The single quotes must match (an even number) and the characters between the single quotes are considered quoted. This is the behavior of POSIX mode through version 4.1. The default Bash behavior remains as in previous versions.

compat42   If set, Bash does not process the replacement string in the pattern substitution word expansion using quote removal.

compat43   If set, Bash does not print a warning message if an attempt is made to use a quoted compound array assignment as an argument to **declare**, makes word expansion errors non-fatal errors that cause the current command to fail (the default behavior is to make them fatal errors that cause the shell to exit), and does not reset the loop state when a shell function is executed (this allows **break** or **continue** in a shell function to affect loops in the caller's context).

complete_fullquote

If set, Bash quotes all shell metacharacters in filenames and directory names when performing completion. If not set, Bash removes metacharacters such as the dollar sign from the set of characters that will be quoted in completed filenames when these metacharacters appear in shell variable references in words to be completed. This means that dollar signs in variable names that expand to directories will not be quoted; however, any dollar signs appearing in filenames will not be quoted, either. This is active only when bash is using backslashes to quote completed filenames. This variable is set by default, which is the default Bash behavior in versions through 4.2.

direxpand

If set, Bash replaces directory names with the results of word expansion when performing filename completion. This changes the contents of the readline editing buffer. If not set, Bash attempts to preserve what the user typed.

dirspell   If set, Bash attempts spelling correction on directory names during word completion if the directory name initially supplied does not exist.

dotglob   If set, Bash includes filenames beginning with a '.' in the results of filename expansion.

execfail   If this is set, a non-interactive shell will not exit if it cannot execute the file specified as an argument to the **exec** builtin command. An interactive shell does not exit if **exec** fails.

expand_aliases

If set, aliases are expanded as described below under Aliases, Section 6.6 [Aliases], page 90. This option is enabled by default for interactive shells.

extdebug   If set at shell invocation, arrange to execute the debugger profile
            before the shell starts, identical to the `--debugger` option. If set
            after invocation, behavior intended for use by debuggers is enabled:

    1. The `-F` option to the `declare` builtin (see Section 4.2 [Bash
       Builtins], page 49) displays the source file name and line num-
       ber corresponding to each function name supplied as an argu-
       ment.

    2. If the command run by the `DEBUG` trap returns a non-zero value,
       the next command is skipped and not executed.

    3. If the command run by the `DEBUG` trap returns a value of 2,
       and the shell is executing in a subroutine (a shell function or
       a shell script executed by the `.` or `source` builtins), the shell
       simulates a call to `return`.

    4. `BASH_ARGC` and `BASH_ARGV` are updated as described in their
       descriptions (see Section 5.2 [Bash Variables], page 71).

    5. Function tracing is enabled: command substitution, shell
       functions, and subshells invoked with (*command*) inherit the
       `DEBUG` and `RETURN` traps.

    6. Error tracing is enabled: command substitution, shell func-
       tions, and subshells invoked with (*command*) inherit the `ERR`
       trap.

extglob   If set, the extended pattern matching features described above (see
            Section 3.5.8.1 [Pattern Matching], page 31) are enabled.

extquote   If set, `$'`*string*`'` and `$"`*string*`"` quoting is performed within
            `${`*parameter*`}` expansions enclosed in double quotes. This option
            is enabled by default.

failglob   If set, patterns which fail to match filenames during filename ex-
            pansion result in an expansion error.

force_fignore

            If set, the suffixes specified by the `FIGNORE` shell variable cause
            words to be ignored when performing word completion even if the
            ignored words are the only possible completions. See Section 5.2
            [Bash Variables], page 71, for a description of `FIGNORE`. This option
            is enabled by default.

globasciiranges

            If set, range expressions used in pattern matching bracket expres-
            sions (see Section 3.5.8.1 [Pattern Matching], page 31) behave as if
            in the traditional C locale when performing comparisons. That is,
            the current locale's collating sequence is not taken into account, so
            'b' will not collate between 'A' and 'B', and upper-case and lower-
            case ASCII characters will collate together.

globstar   If set, the pattern '**' used in a filename expansion context will
            match all files and zero or more directories and subdirectories. If

the pattern is followed by a '/', only directories and subdirectories match.

gnu_errfmt

If set, shell error messages are written in the standard GNU error message format.

histappend

If set, the history list is appended to the file named by the value of the HISTFILE variable when the shell exits, rather than overwriting the file.

histreedit

If set, and Readline is being used, a user is given the opportunity to re-edit a failed history substitution.

histverify

If set, and Readline is being used, the results of history substitution are not immediately passed to the shell parser. Instead, the resulting line is loaded into the Readline editing buffer, allowing further modification.

hostcomplete

If set, and Readline is being used, Bash will attempt to perform hostname completion when a word containing a '@' is being completed (see Section 8.4.6 [Commands For Completion], page 124). This option is enabled by default.

huponexit

If set, Bash will send SIGHUP to all jobs when an interactive login shell exits (see Section 3.7.6 [Signals], page 39).

inherit_errexit

If set, command substitution inherits the value of the errexit option, instead of unsetting it in the subshell environment. This option is enabled when POSIX mode is enabled.

interactive_comments

Allow a word beginning with '#' to cause that word and all remaining characters on that line to be ignored in an interactive shell. This option is enabled by default.

lastpipe   If set, and job control is not active, the shell runs the last command of a pipeline not executed in the background in the current shell environment.

lithist   If enabled, and the cmdhist option is enabled, multi-line commands are saved to the history with embedded newlines rather than using semicolon separators where possible.

login_shell

The shell sets this option if it is started as a login shell (see Section 6.1 [Invoking Bash], page 82). The value may not be changed.

mailwarn   If set, and a file that Bash is checking for mail has been accessed since the last time it was checked, the message `"The mail in mailfile has been read"` is displayed.

no_empty_cmd_completion

If set, and Readline is being used, Bash will not attempt to search the `PATH` for possible completions when completion is attempted on an empty line.

nocaseglob

If set, Bash matches filenames in a case-insensitive fashion when performing filename expansion.

nocasematch

If set, Bash matches patterns in a case-insensitive fashion when performing matching while executing `case` or `[[` conditional commands, when performing pattern substitution word expansions, or when filtering possible completions as part of programmable completion.

nullglob   If set, Bash allows filename patterns which match no files to expand to a null string, rather than themselves.

progcomp   If set, the programmable completion facilities (see Section 8.6 [Programmable Completion], page 129) are enabled. This option is enabled by default.

promptvars

If set, prompt strings undergo parameter expansion, command substitution, arithmetic expansion, and quote removal after being expanded as described below (see Section 6.9 [Controlling the Prompt], page 94). This option is enabled by default.

restricted_shell

The shell sets this option if it is started in restricted mode (see Section 6.10 [The Restricted Shell], page 95). The value may not be changed. This is not reset when the startup files are executed, allowing the startup files to discover whether or not a shell is restricted.

shift_verbose

If this is set, the `shift` builtin prints an error message when the shift count exceeds the number of positional parameters.

sourcepath

If set, the `source` builtin uses the value of `PATH` to find the directory containing the file supplied as an argument. This option is enabled by default.

xpg_echo   If set, the `echo` builtin expands backslash-escape sequences by default.

The return status when listing options is zero if all *optnames* are enabled, non-zero otherwise. When setting or unsetting options, the return status is zero unless an *optname* is not a valid shell option.

4.4 Special Builtins

For historical reasons, the POSIX standard has classified several builtin commands as *special*. When Bash is executing in POSIX mode, the special builtins differ from other builtin commands in three respects:

1. Special builtins are found before shell functions during command lookup.

2. If a special builtin returns an error status, a non-interactive shell exits.

3. Assignment statements preceding the command stay in effect in the shell environment after the command completes.

When Bash is not executing in POSIX mode, these builtins behave no differently than the rest of the Bash builtin commands. The Bash POSIX mode is described in Section 6.11 [Bash POSIX Mode], page 96.

These are the POSIX special builtins:

```
break : . continue eval exec exit export readonly return set
shift trap unset
```

5 Shell Variables

This chapter describes the shell variables that Bash uses. Bash automatically assigns default values to a number of variables.

5.1 Bourne Shell Variables

Bash uses certain shell variables in the same way as the Bourne shell. In some cases, Bash assigns a default value to the variable.

CDPATH   A colon-separated list of directories used as a search path for the `cd` builtin command.

HOME   The current user's home directory; the default for the `cd` builtin command. The value of this variable is also used by tilde expansion (see Section 3.5.2 [Tilde Expansion], page 22).

IFS   A list of characters that separate fields; used when the shell splits words as part of expansion.

MAIL   If this parameter is set to a filename or directory name and the `MAILPATH` variable is not set, Bash informs the user of the arrival of mail in the specified file or Maildir-format directory.

MAILPATH   A colon-separated list of filenames which the shell periodically checks for new mail. Each list entry can specify the message that is printed when new mail arrives in the mail file by separating the filename from the message with a '?'. When used in the text of the message, `$_` expands to the name of the current mail file.

OPTARG   The value of the last option argument processed by the `getopts` builtin.

OPTIND   The index of the last option argument processed by the `getopts` builtin.

PATH   A colon-separated list of directories in which the shell looks for commands. A zero-length (null) directory name in the value of `PATH` indicates the current directory. A null directory name may appear as two adjacent colons, or as an initial or trailing colon.

PS1   The primary prompt string. The default value is '\s-\v\$ '. See Section 6.9 [Controlling the Prompt], page 94, for the complete list of escape sequences that are expanded before `PS1` is displayed.

PS2   The secondary prompt string. The default value is '> '.

5.2 Bash Variables

These variables are set or used by Bash, but other shells do not normally treat them specially.

A few variables used by Bash are described in different chapters: variables for controlling the job control facilities (see Section 7.3 [Job Control Variables], page 103).

BASH   The full pathname used to execute the current instance of Bash.

BASHOPTS   A colon-separated list of enabled shell options. Each word in the list is a valid argument for the -s option to the shopt builtin command (see Section 4.3.2 [The Shopt Builtin], page 64). The options appearing in BASHOPTS are those reported as 'on' by 'shopt'. If this variable is in the environment when Bash starts up, each shell option in the list will be enabled before reading any startup files. This variable is readonly.

BASHPID   Expands to the process ID of the current Bash process. This differs from $$ under certain circumstances, such as subshells that do not require Bash to be re-initialized.

BASH_ALIASES
            An associative array variable whose members correspond to the internal list of aliases as maintained by the alias builtin. (see Section 4.1 [Bourne Shell Builtins], page 42). Elements added to this array appear in the alias list; however, unsetting array elements currently does not cause aliases to be removed from the alias list. If BASH_ALIASES is unset, it loses its special properties, even if it is subsequently reset.

BASH_ARGC
            An array variable whose values are the number of parameters in each frame of the current bash execution call stack. The number of parameters to the current subroutine (shell function or script executed with . or source) is at the top of the stack. When a subroutine is executed, the number of parameters passed is pushed onto BASH_ARGC. The shell sets BASH_ARGC only when in extended debugging mode (see Section 4.3.2 [The Shopt Builtin], page 64, for a description of the extdebug option to the shopt builtin).

BASH_ARGV
            An array variable containing all of the parameters in the current bash execution call stack. The final parameter of the last subroutine call is at the top of the stack; the first parameter of the initial call is at the bottom. When a subroutine is executed, the parameters supplied are pushed onto BASH_ARGV. The shell sets BASH_ARGV only when in extended debugging mode (see Section 4.3.2 [The Shopt Builtin], page 64, for a description of the extdebug option to the shopt builtin).

BASH_CMDS
            An associative array variable whose members correspond to the internal hash table of commands as maintained by the hash builtin (see Section 4.1 [Bourne Shell Builtins], page 42). Elements added to this array appear in the hash table; however, unsetting array elements currently does not cause command names to be removed from the hash table. If BASH_CMDS is unset, it loses its special properties, even if it is subsequently reset.

BASH_COMMAND
            The command currently being executed or about to be executed, unless the shell is executing a command as the result of a trap, in which case it is the command executing at the time of the trap.

BASH_COMPAT
        The value is used to set the shell's compatibility level. See Section 4.3.2 [The Shopt Builtin], page 64, for a description of the various compatibility levels and their effects. The value may be a decimal number (e.g., 4.2) or an integer (e.g., 42) corresponding to the desired compatibility level. If `BASH_COMPAT` is unset or set to the empty string, the compatibility level is set to the default for the current version. If `BASH_COMPAT` is set to a value that is not one of the valid compatibility levels, the shell prints an error message and sets the compatibility level to the default for the current version. The valid compatibility levels correspond to the compatibility options accepted by the **shopt** builtin described above (for example, *compat42* means that 4.2 and 42 are valid values). The current version is also a valid value.

BASH_ENV   If this variable is set when Bash is invoked to execute a shell script, its value is expanded and used as the name of a startup file to read before executing the script. See Section 6.2 [Bash Startup Files], page 84.

BASH_EXECUTION_STRING
        The command argument to the -c invocation option.

BASH_LINENO
        An array variable whose members are the line numbers in source files where each corresponding member of *FUNCNAME* was invoked. `${BASH_LINENO[$i]}` is the line number in the source file (`${BASH_SOURCE[$i+1]}`) where `${FUNCNAME[$i]}` was called (or `${BASH_LINENO[$i-1]}` if referenced within another shell function). Use `LINENO` to obtain the current line number.

BASH_LOADABLES_PATH
        A colon-separated list of directories in which the shell looks for dynamically loadable builtins specified by the **enable** command.

BASH_REMATCH
        An array variable whose members are assigned by the '=~' binary operator to the [[conditional command (see Section 3.2.4.2 [Conditional Constructs], page 10). The element with index 0 is the portion of the string matching the entire regular expression. The element with index *n* is the portion of the string matching the *n*th parenthesized subexpression. This variable is read-only.

BASH_SOURCE
        An array variable whose members are the source filenames where the corresponding shell function names in the `FUNCNAME` array variable are defined. The shell function `${FUNCNAME[$i]}` is defined in the file `${BASH_SOURCE[$i]}` and called from `${BASH_SOURCE[$i+1]}`

BASH_SUBSHELL
        Incremented by one within each subshell or subshell environment when the shell begins executing in that environment. The initial value is 0.

BASH_VERSINFO
        A readonly array variable (see Section 6.7 [Arrays], page 91) whose members hold version information for this instance of Bash. The values assigned to the array members are as follows:

BASH_VERSINFO[0]
> The major version number (the *release*).

BASH_VERSINFO[1]
> The minor version number (the *version*).

BASH_VERSINFO[2]
> The patch level.

BASH_VERSINFO[3]
> The build version.

BASH_VERSINFO[4]
> The release status (e.g., *beta1*).

BASH_VERSINFO[5]
> The value of MACHTYPE.

BASH_VERSION
> The version number of the current instance of Bash.

BASH_XTRACEFD
> If set to an integer corresponding to a valid file descriptor, Bash will write the trace output generated when 'set -x' is enabled to that file descriptor. This allows tracing output to be separated from diagnostic and error messages. The file descriptor is closed when BASH_XTRACEFD is unset or assigned a new value. Unsetting BASH_XTRACEFD or assigning it the empty string causes the trace output to be sent to the standard error. Note that setting BASH_XTRACEFD to 2 (the standard error file descriptor) and then unsetting it will result in the standard error being closed.

CHILD_MAX
> Set the number of exited child status values for the shell to remember. Bash will not allow this value to be decreased below a POSIX-mandated minimum, and there is a maximum value (currently 8192) that this may not exceed. The minimum value is system-dependent.

COLUMNS
> Used by the **select** command to determine the terminal width when printing selection lists. Automatically set if the **checkwinsize** option is enabled (see Section 4.3.2 [The Shopt Builtin], page 64), or in an interactive shell upon receipt of a SIGWINCH.

COMP_CWORD
> An index into ${COMP_WORDS} of the word containing the current cursor position. This variable is available only in shell functions invoked by the programmable completion facilities (see Section 8.6 [Programmable Completion], page 129).

COMP_LINE
> The current command line. This variable is available only in shell functions and external commands invoked by the programmable completion facilities (see Section 8.6 [Programmable Completion], page 129).

COMP_POINT
> The index of the current cursor position relative to the beginning of the current command. If the current cursor position is at the end of the current command, the value of this variable is equal to ${#COMP_LINE}. This variable is available only in shell functions and external commands invoked by the programmable completion facilities (see Section 8.6 [Programmable Completion], page 129).

COMP_TYPE
> Set to an integer value corresponding to the type of completion attempted that caused a completion function to be called: *TAB*, for normal completion, '?', for listing completions after successive tabs, '!', for listing alternatives on partial word completion, '@', to list completions if the word is not unmodified, or '%', for menu completion. This variable is available only in shell functions and external commands invoked by the programmable completion facilities (see Section 8.6 [Programmable Completion], page 129).

COMP_KEY   The key (or final key of a key sequence) used to invoke the current completion function.

COMP_WORDBREAKS
> The set of characters that the Readline library treats as word separators when performing word completion. If COMP_WORDBREAKS is unset, it loses its special properties, even if it is subsequently reset.

COMP_WORDS
> An array variable consisting of the individual words in the current command line. The line is split into words as Readline would split it, using COMP_WORDBREAKS as described above. This variable is available only in shell functions invoked by the programmable completion facilities (see Section 8.6 [Programmable Completion], page 129).

COMPREPLY
> An array variable from which Bash reads the possible completions generated by a shell function invoked by the programmable completion facility (see Section 8.6 [Programmable Completion], page 129). Each array element contains one possible completion.

COPROC   An array variable created to hold the file descriptors for output from and input to an unnamed coprocess (see Section 3.2.5 [Coprocesses], page 15).

DIRSTACK   An array variable containing the current contents of the directory stack. Directories appear in the stack in the order they are displayed by the dirs builtin. Assigning to members of this array variable may be used to modify directories already in the stack, but the pushd and popd builtins must be used to add and remove directories. Assignment to this variable will not change the current directory. If DIRSTACK is unset, it loses its special properties, even if it is subsequently reset.

EMACS   If Bash finds this variable in the environment when the shell starts with value 't', it assumes that the shell is running in an Emacs shell buffer and disables line editing.

ENV   Similar to `BASH_ENV`; used when the shell is invoked in POSIX Mode (see
                Section 6.11 [Bash POSIX Mode], page 96).

EUID   The numeric effective user id of the current user. This variable is readonly.

EXECIGNORE
                A colon-separated list of shell patterns (see Section 3.5.8.1 [Pattern Matching],
                page 31) defining the list of filenames to be ignored by command search using
                `PATH`. Files whose full pathnames match one of these patterns are not considered
                executable files for the purposes of completion and command execution via `PATH`
                lookup. This does not affect the behavior of the `[`, `test`, and `[[` commands.
                Full pathnames in the command hash table are not subject to `EXECIGNORE`.
                Use this variable to ignore shared library files that have the executable bit set,
                but are not executable files. The pattern matching honors the setting of the
                `extglob` shell option.

FCEDIT   The editor used as a default by the `-e` option to the `fc` builtin command.

FIGNORE   A colon-separated list of suffixes to ignore when performing filename comple-
                tion. A filename whose suffix matches one of the entries in `FIGNORE` is excluded
                from the list of matched filenames. A sample value is '`.o:~`'

FUNCNAME   An array variable containing the names of all shell functions currently in the
                execution call stack. The element with index 0 is the name of any currently-
                executing shell function. The bottom-most element (the one with the highest
                index) is `"main"`. This variable exists only when a shell function is executing.
                Assignments to `FUNCNAME` have no effect. If `FUNCNAME` is unset, it loses its special
                properties, even if it is subsequently reset.

                This variable can be used with `BASH_LINENO` and `BASH_SOURCE`. Each element
                of `FUNCNAME` has corresponding elements in `BASH_LINENO` and `BASH_SOURCE` to
                describe the call stack. For instance, `${FUNCNAME[$i]}` was called from the
                file `${BASH_SOURCE[$i+1]}` at line number `${BASH_LINENO[$i]}`. The `caller`
                builtin displays the current call stack using this information.

FUNCNEST   If set to a numeric value greater than 0, defines a maximum function nesting
                level. Function invocations that exceed this nesting level will cause the current
                command to abort.

GLOBIGNORE
                A colon-separated list of patterns defining the set of filenames to be ignored
                by filename expansion. If a filename matched by a filename expansion pattern
                also matches one of the patterns in `GLOBIGNORE`, it is removed from the list of
                matches. The pattern matching honors the setting of the `extglob` shell option.

GROUPS   An array variable containing the list of groups of which the current user is a
                member. Assignments to `GROUPS` have no effect. If `GROUPS` is unset, it loses its
                special properties, even if it is subsequently reset.

histchars
                Up to three characters which control history expansion, quick substitution, and
                tokenization (see Section 9.3 [History Interaction], page 139). The first charac-
                ter is the *history expansion* character, that is, the character which signifies the

start of a history expansion, normally '!'. The second character is the character which signifies 'quick substitution' when seen as the first character on a line, normally '^'. The optional third character is the character which indicates that the remainder of the line is a comment when found as the first character of a word, usually '#'. The history comment character causes history substitution to be skipped for the remaining words on the line. It does not necessarily cause the shell parser to treat the rest of the line as a comment.

HISTCMD   The history number, or index in the history list, of the current command. If HISTCMD is unset, it loses its special properties, even if it is subsequently reset.

HISTCONTROL
A colon-separated list of values controlling how commands are saved on the history list. If the list of values includes 'ignorespace', lines which begin with a space character are not saved in the history list. A value of 'ignoredups' causes lines which match the previous history entry to not be saved. A value of 'ignoreboth' is shorthand for 'ignorespace' and 'ignoredups'. A value of 'erasedups' causes all previous lines matching the current line to be removed from the history list before that line is saved. Any value not in the above list is ignored. If HISTCONTROL is unset, or does not include a valid value, all lines read by the shell parser are saved on the history list, subject to the value of HISTIGNORE. The second and subsequent lines of a multi-line compound command are not tested, and are added to the history regardless of the value of HISTCONTROL.

HISTFILE   The name of the file to which the command history is saved. The default value is ~/.bash_history.

HISTFILESIZE
The maximum number of lines contained in the history file. When this variable is assigned a value, the history file is truncated, if necessary, to contain no more than that number of lines by removing the oldest entries. The history file is also truncated to this size after writing it when a shell exits. If the value is 0, the history file is truncated to zero size. Non-numeric values and numeric values less than zero inhibit truncation. The shell sets the default value to the value of HISTSIZE after reading any startup files.

HISTIGNORE
A colon-separated list of patterns used to decide which command lines should be saved on the history list. Each pattern is anchored at the beginning of the line and must match the complete line (no implicit '*' is appended). Each pattern is tested against the line after the checks specified by HISTCONTROL are applied. In addition to the normal shell pattern matching characters, '&' matches the previous history line. '&' may be escaped using a backslash; the backslash is removed before attempting a match. The second and subsequent lines of a multi-line compound command are not tested, and are added to the history regardless of the value of HISTIGNORE. The pattern matching honors the setting of the extglob shell option.

HISTIGNORE subsumes the function of HISTCONTROL. A pattern of '&' is identical to ignoredups, and a pattern of '[ ]*' is identical to ignorespace. Combining these two patterns, separating them with a colon, provides the functionality of `ignoreboth`.

HISTSIZE   The maximum number of commands to remember on the history list. If the value is 0, commands are not saved in the history list. Numeric values less than zero result in every command being saved on the history list (there is no limit). The shell sets the default value to 500 after reading any startup files.

HISTTIMEFORMAT
            If this variable is set and not null, its value is used as a format string for *strftime* to print the time stamp associated with each history entry displayed by the `history` builtin. If this variable is set, time stamps are written to the history file so they may be preserved across shell sessions. This uses the history comment character to distinguish timestamps from other history lines.

HOSTFILE   Contains the name of a file in the same format as `/etc/hosts` that should be read when the shell needs to complete a hostname. The list of possible hostname completions may be changed while the shell is running; the next time hostname completion is attempted after the value is changed, Bash adds the contents of the new file to the existing list. If `HOSTFILE` is set, but has no value, or does not name a readable file, Bash attempts to read `/etc/hosts` to obtain the list of possible hostname completions. When `HOSTFILE` is unset, the hostname list is cleared.

HOSTNAME   The name of the current host.

HOSTTYPE   A string describing the machine Bash is running on.

IGNOREEOF
            Controls the action of the shell on receipt of an `EOF` character as the sole input. If set, the value denotes the number of consecutive `EOF` characters that can be read as the first character on an input line before the shell will exit. If the variable exists but does not have a numeric value (or has no value) then the default is 10. If the variable does not exist, then `EOF` signifies the end of input to the shell. This is only in effect for interactive shells.

INPUTRC   The name of the Readline initialization file, overriding the default of `~/.inputrc`.

LANG   Used to determine the locale category for any category not specifically selected with a variable starting with `LC_`.

LC_ALL   This variable overrides the value of `LANG` and any other `LC_` variable specifying a locale category.

LC_COLLATE
            This variable determines the collation order used when sorting the results of filename expansion, and determines the behavior of range expressions, equivalence classes, and collating sequences within filename expansion and pattern matching (see Section 3.5.8 [Filename Expansion], page 30).

LC_CTYPE   This variable determines the interpretation of characters and the behavior of character classes within filename expansion and pattern matching (see Section 3.5.8 [Filename Expansion], page 30).

LC_MESSAGES
>   This variable determines the locale used to translate double-quoted strings preceded by a '$' (see Section 3.1.2.5 [Locale Translation], page 7).

LC_NUMERIC
>   This variable determines the locale category used for number formatting.

LC_TIME   This variable determines the locale category used for data and time formatting.

LINENO   The line number in the script or shell function currently executing.

LINES   Used by the **select** command to determine the column length for printing selection lists. Automatically set if the **checkwinsize** option is enabled (see Section 4.3.2 [The Shopt Builtin], page 64), or in an interactive shell upon receipt of a SIGWINCH.

MACHTYPE   A string that fully describes the system type on which Bash is executing, in the standard GNU *cpu-company-system* format.

MAILCHECK
>   How often (in seconds) that the shell should check for mail in the files specified in the MAILPATH or MAIL variables. The default is 60 seconds. When it is time to check for mail, the shell does so before displaying the primary prompt. If this variable is unset, or set to a value that is not a number greater than or equal to zero, the shell disables mail checking.

MAPFILE   An array variable created to hold the text read by the **mapfile** builtin when no variable name is supplied.

OLDPWD   The previous working directory as set by the **cd** builtin.

OPTERR   If set to the value 1, Bash displays error messages generated by the **getopts** builtin command.

OSTYPE   A string describing the operating system Bash is running on.

PIPESTATUS
>   An array variable (see Section 6.7 [Arrays], page 91) containing a list of exit status values from the processes in the most-recently-executed foreground pipeline (which may contain only a single command).

POSIXLY_CORRECT
>   If this variable is in the environment when Bash starts, the shell enters POSIX mode (see Section 6.11 [Bash POSIX Mode], page 96) before reading the startup files, as if the **--posix** invocation option had been supplied. If it is set while the shell is running, Bash enables POSIX mode, as if the command

```
set -o posix
```

>   had been executed.

PPID   The process ID of the shell's parent process. This variable is readonly.

PROMPT_COMMAND
>   If set, the value is interpreted as a command to execute before the printing of each primary prompt ($PS1).

PROMPT_DIRTRIM

> If set to a number greater than zero, the value is used as the number of trailing directory components to retain when expanding the \w and \W prompt string escapes (see Section 6.9 [Controlling the Prompt], page 94). Characters removed are replaced with an ellipsis.

PS0

> The value of this parameter is expanded like *PS1* and displayed by interactive shells after reading a command and before the command is executed.

PS3

> The value of this variable is used as the prompt for the `select` command. If this variable is not set, the `select` command prompts with '#? '

PS4

> The value is the prompt printed before the command line is echoed when the -x option is set (see Section 4.3.1 [The Set Builtin], page 60). The first character of PS4 is replicated multiple times, as necessary, to indicate multiple levels of indirection. The default is '+ '.

PWD

> The current working directory as set by the `cd` builtin.

RANDOM

> Each time this parameter is referenced, a random integer between 0 and 32767 is generated. Assigning a value to this variable seeds the random number generator.

READLINE_LINE

> The contents of the Readline line buffer, for use with 'bind -x' (see Section 4.2 [Bash Builtins], page 49).

READLINE_POINT

> The position of the insertion point in the Readline line buffer, for use with 'bind -x' (see Section 4.2 [Bash Builtins], page 49).

REPLY

> The default variable for the `read` builtin.

SECONDS

> This variable expands to the number of seconds since the shell was started. Assignment to this variable resets the count to the value assigned, and the expanded value becomes the value assigned plus the number of seconds since the assignment.

SHELL

> The full pathname to the shell is kept in this environment variable. If it is not set when the shell starts, Bash assigns to it the full pathname of the current user's login shell.

SHELLOPTS

> A colon-separated list of enabled shell options. Each word in the list is a valid argument for the -o option to the `set` builtin command (see Section 4.3.1 [The Set Builtin], page 60). The options appearing in SHELLOPTS are those reported as 'on' by 'set -o'. If this variable is in the environment when Bash starts up, each shell option in the list will be enabled before reading any startup files. This variable is readonly.

SHLVL

> Incremented by one each time a new instance of Bash is started. This is intended to be a count of how deeply your Bash shells are nested.

TIMEFORMAT

> The value of this parameter is used as a format string specifying how the timing information for pipelines prefixed with the `time` reserved word should be displayed. The '%' character introduces an escape sequence that is expanded to a time value or other information. The escape sequences and their meanings are as follows; the braces denote optional portions.
>
> %%   A literal '%'.
>
> %[p][l]R   The elapsed time in seconds.
>
> %[p][l]U   The number of CPU seconds spent in user mode.
>
> %[p][l]S   The number of CPU seconds spent in system mode.
>
> %P   The CPU percentage, computed as (%U + %S) / %R.
>
> The optional p is a digit specifying the precision, the number of fractional digits after a decimal point. A value of 0 causes no decimal point or fraction to be output. At most three places after the decimal point may be specified; values of p greater than 3 are changed to 3. If p is not specified, the value 3 is used.
>
> The optional l specifies a longer format, including minutes, of the form MMmSS.FFs. The value of p determines whether or not the fraction is included.
>
> If this variable is not set, Bash acts as if it had the value
>
> > $'\nreal\t%3lR\nuser\t%3lU\nsys\t%3lS'
>
> If the value is null, no timing information is displayed. A trailing newline is added when the format string is displayed.

TMOUT

> If set to a value greater than zero, `TMOUT` is treated as the default timeout for the `read` builtin (see Section 4.2 [Bash Builtins], page 49). The `select` command (see Section 3.2.4.2 [Conditional Constructs], page 10) terminates if input does not arrive after `TMOUT` seconds when input is coming from a terminal.
>
> In an interactive shell, the value is interpreted as the number of seconds to wait for a line of input after issuing the primary prompt. Bash terminates after waiting for that number of seconds if a complete line of input does not arrive.

TMPDIR

> If set, Bash uses its value as the name of a directory in which Bash creates temporary files for the shell's use.

UID

> The numeric real user id of the current user. This variable is readonly.

6 Bash Features

This chapter describes features unique to Bash.

6.1 Invoking Bash

```
bash [long-opt] [-ir] [-abefhkmnptuvxdBCDHP] [-o option] [-O shopt_option] [ar-
gument ...]
bash [long-opt] [-abefhkmnptuvxdBCDHP] [-o option] [-O shopt_option] -c string [ar-
gument ...]
bash [long-opt] -s [-abefhkmnptuvxdBCDHP] [-o option] [-O shopt_option] [ar-
gument ...]
```

All of the single-character options used with the **set** builtin (see Section 4.3.1 [The Set Builtin], page 60) can be used as options when the shell is invoked. In addition, there are several multi-character options that you can use. These options must appear on the command line before the single-character options to be recognized.

`--debugger`

Arrange for the debugger profile to be executed before the shell starts. Turns on extended debugging mode (see Section 4.3.2 [The Shopt Builtin], page 64, for a description of the **extdebug** option to the **shopt** builtin).

`--dump-po-strings`

A list of all double-quoted strings preceded by '$' is printed on the standard output in the GNU **gettext** PO (portable object) file format. Equivalent to -D except for the output format.

`--dump-strings`

Equivalent to -D.

`--help`   Display a usage message on standard output and exit successfully.

`--init-file` *filename*
`--rcfile` *filename*

Execute commands from *filename* (instead of ~/.bashrc) in an interactive shell.

`--login`   Equivalent to -l.

`--noediting`

Do not use the GNU Readline library (see Chapter 8 [Command Line Editing], page 104) to read command lines when the shell is interactive.

`--noprofile`

Don't load the system-wide startup file /etc/profile or any of the personal initialization files ~/.bash_profile, ~/.bash_login, or ~/.profile when Bash is invoked as a login shell.

`--norc`   Don't read the ~/.bashrc initialization file in an interactive shell. This is on by default if the shell is invoked as **sh**.

`--posix`   Change the behavior of Bash where the default operation differs from the POSIX standard to match the standard. This is intended to make Bash behave as a strict superset of that standard. See Section 6.11 [Bash POSIX Mode], page 96, for a description of the Bash POSIX mode.

`--restricted`

>Make the shell a restricted shell (see Section 6.10 [The Restricted Shell], page 95).

`--verbose`

>Equivalent to `-v`. Print shell input lines as they're read.

`--version`

>Show version information for this instance of Bash on the standard output and exit successfully.

There are several single-character options that may be supplied at invocation which are not available with the `set` builtin.

`-c`
>Read and execute commands from the first non-option argument *command_string*, then exit. If there are arguments after the *command_string*, the first argument is assigned to `$0` and any remaining arguments are assigned to the positional parameters. The assignment to `$0` sets the name of the shell, which is used in warning and error messages.

`-i`
>Force the shell to run interactively. Interactive shells are described in Section 6.3 [Interactive Shells], page 85.

`-l`
>Make this shell act as if it had been directly invoked by login. When the shell is interactive, this is equivalent to starting a login shell with '`exec -l bash`'. When the shell is not interactive, the login shell startup files will be executed. '`exec bash -l`' or '`exec bash --login`' will replace the current shell with a Bash login shell. See Section 6.2 [Bash Startup Files], page 84, for a description of the special behavior of a login shell.

`-r`
>Make the shell a restricted shell (see Section 6.10 [The Restricted Shell], page 95).

`-s`
>If this option is present, or if no arguments remain after option processing, then commands are read from the standard input. This option allows the positional parameters to be set when invoking an interactive shell.

`-D`
>A list of all double-quoted strings preceded by '`$`' is printed on the standard output. These are the strings that are subject to language translation when the current locale is not `C` or `POSIX` (see Section 3.1.2.5 [Locale Translation], page 7). This implies the `-n` option; no commands will be executed.

`[-+]O [shopt_option]`
>*shopt_option* is one of the shell options accepted by the `shopt` builtin (see Section 4.3.2 [The Shopt Builtin], page 64). If *shopt_option* is present, `-O` sets the value of that option; `+O` unsets it. If *shopt_option* is not supplied, the names and values of the shell options accepted by `shopt` are printed on the standard output. If the invocation option is `+O`, the output is displayed in a format that may be reused as input.

`--`
>A `--` signals the end of options and disables further option processing. Any arguments after the `--` are treated as filenames and arguments.

A *login* shell is one whose first character of argument zero is '-', or one invoked with the `--login` option.

An *interactive* shell is one started without non-option arguments, unless `-s` is specified, without specifying the `-c` option, and whose input and output are both connected to terminals (as determined by `isatty(3)`), or one started with the `-i` option. See Section 6.3 [Interactive Shells], page 85, for more information.

If arguments remain after option processing, and neither the `-c` nor the `-s` option has been supplied, the first argument is assumed to be the name of a file containing shell commands (see Section 3.8 [Shell Scripts], page 40). When Bash is invoked in this fashion, `$0` is set to the name of the file, and the positional parameters are set to the remaining arguments. Bash reads and executes commands from this file, then exits. Bash's exit status is the exit status of the last command executed in the script. If no commands are executed, the exit status is 0.

6.2 Bash Startup Files

This section describes how Bash executes its startup files. If any of the files exist but cannot be read, Bash reports an error. Tildes are expanded in filenames as described above under Tilde Expansion (see Section 3.5.2 [Tilde Expansion], page 22).

Interactive shells are described in Section 6.3 [Interactive Shells], page 85.

Invoked as an interactive login shell, or with `--login`

When Bash is invoked as an interactive login shell, or as a non-interactive shell with the `--login` option, it first reads and executes commands from the file `/etc/profile`, if that file exists. After reading that file, it looks for `~/.bash_profile`, `~/.bash_login`, and `~/.profile`, in that order, and reads and executes commands from the first one that exists and is readable. The `--noprofile` option may be used when the shell is started to inhibit this behavior.

When an interactive login shell exits, or a non-interactive login shell executes the `exit` builtin command, Bash reads and executes commands from the file `~/.bash_logout`, if it exists.

Invoked as an interactive non-login shell

When an interactive shell that is not a login shell is started, Bash reads and executes commands from `~/.bashrc`, if that file exists. This may be inhibited by using the `--norc` option. The `--rcfile file` option will force Bash to read and execute commands from *file* instead of `~/.bashrc`.

So, typically, your `~/.bash_profile` contains the line

```
if [ -f ~/.bashrc ]; then . ~/.bashrc; fi
```

after (or before) any login-specific initializations.

Invoked non-interactively

When Bash is started non-interactively, to run a shell script, for example, it looks for the variable `BASH_ENV` in the environment, expands its value if it appears there, and uses the expanded value as the name of a file to read and execute. Bash behaves as if the following command were executed:

```
if [ -n "$BASH_ENV" ]; then . "$BASH_ENV"; fi
```

but the value of the `PATH` variable is not used to search for the filename.

As noted above, if a non-interactive shell is invoked with the `--login` option, Bash attempts to read and execute commands from the login shell startup files.

Invoked with name `sh`

If Bash is invoked with the name `sh`, it tries to mimic the startup behavior of historical versions of `sh` as closely as possible, while conforming to the POSIX standard as well.

When invoked as an interactive login shell, or as a non-interactive shell with the `--login` option, it first attempts to read and execute commands from `/etc/profile` and `~/.profile`, in that order. The `--noprofile` option may be used to inhibit this behavior. When invoked as an interactive shell with the name `sh`, Bash looks for the variable `ENV`, expands its value if it is defined, and uses the expanded value as the name of a file to read and execute. Since a shell invoked as `sh` does not attempt to read and execute commands from any other startup files, the `--rcfile` option has no effect. A non-interactive shell invoked with the name `sh` does not attempt to read any other startup files.

When invoked as `sh`, Bash enters POSIX mode after the startup files are read.

Invoked in POSIX mode

When Bash is started in POSIX mode, as with the `--posix` command line option, it follows the POSIX standard for startup files. In this mode, interactive shells expand the `ENV` variable and commands are read and executed from the file whose name is the expanded value. No other startup files are read.

Invoked by remote shell daemon

Bash attempts to determine when it is being run with its standard input connected to a network connection, as when executed by the remote shell daemon, usually `rshd`, or the secure shell daemon `sshd`. If Bash determines it is being run in this fashion, it reads and executes commands from `~/.bashrc`, if that file exists and is readable. It will not do this if invoked as `sh`. The `--norc` option may be used to inhibit this behavior, and the `--rcfile` option may be used to force another file to be read, but neither `rshd` nor `sshd` generally invoke the shell with those options or allow them to be specified.

Invoked with unequal effective and real UID/GIDs

If Bash is started with the effective user (group) id not equal to the real user (group) id, and the `-p` option is not supplied, no startup files are read, shell functions are not inherited from the environment, the `SHELLOPTS`, `BASHOPTS`, `CDPATH`, and `GLOBIGNORE` variables, if they appear in the environment, are ignored, and the effective user id is set to the real user id. If the `-p` option is supplied at invocation, the startup behavior is the same, but the effective user id is not reset.

6.3 Interactive Shells

6.3.1 What is an Interactive Shell?

An interactive shell is one started without non-option arguments, unless -s is specified, without specifying the -c option, and whose input and error output are both connected to terminals (as determined by isatty(3)), or one started with the -i option.

An interactive shell generally reads from and writes to a user's terminal.

The -s invocation option may be used to set the positional parameters when an interactive shell is started.

6.3.2 Is this Shell Interactive?

To determine within a startup script whether or not Bash is running interactively, test the value of the '-' special parameter. It contains i when the shell is interactive. For example:

```
case "$-" in
*i*) echo This shell is interactive ;;
*) echo This shell is not interactive ;;
esac
```

Alternatively, startup scripts may examine the variable PS1; it is unset in non-interactive shells, and set in interactive shells. Thus:

```
if [ -z "$PS1" ]; then
        echo This shell is not interactive
else
        echo This shell is interactive
fi
```

6.3.3 Interactive Shell Behavior

When the shell is running interactively, it changes its behavior in several ways.

1. Startup files are read and executed as described in Section 6.2 [Bash Startup Files], page 84.

2. Job Control (see Chapter 7 [Job Control], page 100) is enabled by default. When job control is in effect, Bash ignores the keyboard-generated job control signals SIGTTIN, SIGTTOU, and SIGTSTP.

3. Bash expands and displays PS1 before reading the first line of a command, and expands and displays PS2 before reading the second and subsequent lines of a multi-line command. Bash displays PS0 after it reads a command but before executing it.

4. Bash executes the value of the PROMPT_COMMAND variable as a command before printing the primary prompt, $PS1 (see Section 5.2 [Bash Variables], page 71).

5. Readline (see Chapter 8 [Command Line Editing], page 104) is used to read commands from the user's terminal.

6. Bash inspects the value of the ignoreeof option to set -o instead of exiting immediately when it receives an EOF on its standard input when reading a command (see Section 4.3.1 [The Set Builtin], page 60).

7. Command history (see Section 9.1 [Bash History Facilities], page 137) and history expansion (see Section 9.3 [History Interaction], page 139) are enabled by default. Bash will save the command history to the file named by $HISTFILE when a shell with history enabled exits.

8. Alias expansion (see Section 6.6 [Aliases], page 90) is performed by default.

9. In the absence of any traps, Bash ignores `SIGTERM` (see Section 3.7.6 [Signals], page 39).

10. In the absence of any traps, `SIGINT` is caught and handled ((see Section 3.7.6 [Signals], page 39). `SIGINT` will interrupt some shell builtins.

11. An interactive login shell sends a `SIGHUP` to all jobs on exit if the `huponexit` shell option has been enabled (see Section 3.7.6 [Signals], page 39).

12. The `-n` invocation option is ignored, and 'set `-n`' has no effect (see Section 4.3.1 [The Set Builtin], page 60).

13. Bash will check for mail periodically, depending on the values of the `MAIL`, `MAILPATH`, and `MAILCHECK` shell variables (see Section 5.2 [Bash Variables], page 71).

14. Expansion errors due to references to unbound shell variables after 'set `-u`' has been enabled will not cause the shell to exit (see Section 4.3.1 [The Set Builtin], page 60).

15. The shell will not exit on expansion errors caused by *var* being unset or null in `${var:?word}` expansions (see Section 3.5.3 [Shell Parameter Expansion], page 23).

16. Redirection errors encountered by shell builtins will not cause the shell to exit.

17. When running in POSIX mode, a special builtin returning an error status will not cause the shell to exit (see Section 6.11 [Bash POSIX Mode], page 96).

18. A failed `exec` will not cause the shell to exit (see Section 4.1 [Bourne Shell Builtins], page 42).

19. Parser syntax errors will not cause the shell to exit.

20. Simple spelling correction for directory arguments to the `cd` builtin is enabled by default (see the description of the `cdspell` option to the `shopt` builtin in Section 4.3.2 [The Shopt Builtin], page 64).

21. The shell will check the value of the `TMOUT` variable and exit if a command is not read within the specified number of seconds after printing `$PS1` (see Section 5.2 [Bash Variables], page 71).

6.4 Bash Conditional Expressions

Conditional expressions are used by the `[[` compound command and the `test` and `[` builtin commands.

Expressions may be unary or binary. Unary expressions are often used to examine the status of a file. There are string operators and numeric comparison operators as well. Bash handles several filenames specially when they are used in expressions. If the operating system on which Bash is running provides these special files, Bash will use them; otherwise it will emulate them internally with this behavior: If the *file* argument to one of the primaries is of the form `/dev/fd/N`, then file descriptor *N* is checked. If the *file* argument to one of the primaries is one of `/dev/stdin`, `/dev/stdout`, or `/dev/stderr`, file descriptor 0, 1, or 2, respectively, is checked.

When used with `[[`, the '`<`' and '`>`' operators sort lexicographically using the current locale. The `test` command uses ASCII ordering.

Unless otherwise specified, primaries that operate on files follow symbolic links and operate on the target of the link, rather than the link itself.

`-a `*`file`*   True if *file* exists.

-b *file*   True if *file* exists and is a block special file.

-c *file*   True if *file* exists and is a character special file.

-d *file*   True if *file* exists and is a directory.

-e *file*   True if *file* exists.

-f *file*   True if *file* exists and is a regular file.

-g *file*   True if *file* exists and its set-group-id bit is set.

-h *file*   True if *file* exists and is a symbolic link.

-k *file*   True if *file* exists and its "sticky" bit is set.

-p *file*   True if *file* exists and is a named pipe (FIFO).

-r *file*   True if *file* exists and is readable.

-s *file*   True if *file* exists and has a size greater than zero.

-t *fd*   True if file descriptor *fd* is open and refers to a terminal.

-u *file*   True if *file* exists and its set-user-id bit is set.

-w *file*   True if *file* exists and is writable.

-x *file*   True if *file* exists and is executable.

-G *file*   True if *file* exists and is owned by the effective group id.

-L *file*   True if *file* exists and is a symbolic link.

-N *file*   True if *file* exists and has been modified since it was last read.

-O *file*   True if *file* exists and is owned by the effective user id.

-S *file*   True if *file* exists and is a socket.

file1 -ef *file2*
        True if *file1* and *file2* refer to the same device and inode numbers.

file1 -nt *file2*
        True if *file1* is newer (according to modification date) than *file2*, or if *file1* exists
        and *file2* does not.

file1 -ot *file2*
        True if *file1* is older than *file2*, or if *file2* exists and *file1* does not.

-o *optname*
        True if the shell option *optname* is enabled. The list of options appears in
        the description of the -o option to the **set** builtin (see Section 4.3.1 [The Set
        Builtin], page 60).

-v *varname*
        True if the shell variable *varname* is set (has been assigned a value).

-R *varname*
        True if the shell variable *varname* is set and is a name reference.

`-z string`   True if the length of *string* is zero.

`-n string`
`string`   True if the length of *string* is non-zero.

`string1 == string2`
`string1 = string2`
> True if the strings are equal. When used with the `[[` command, this performs pattern matching as described above (see Section 3.2.4.2 [Conditional Constructs], page 10).
>
> '=' should be used with the **test** command for POSIX conformance.

`string1 != string2`
> True if the strings are not equal.

`string1 < string2`
> True if *string1* sorts before *string2* lexicographically.

`string1 > string2`
> True if *string1* sorts after *string2* lexicographically.

`arg1 OP arg2`
> OP is one of '-eq', '-ne', '-lt', '-le', '-gt', or '-ge'. These arithmetic binary operators return true if *arg1* is equal to, not equal to, less than, less than or equal to, greater than, or greater than or equal to *arg2*, respectively. *Arg1* and *arg2* may be positive or negative integers.

6.5 Shell Arithmetic

The shell allows arithmetic expressions to be evaluated, as one of the shell expansions or by using the `((` compound command, the `let` builtin, or the `-i` option to the **declare** builtin.

Evaluation is done in fixed-width integers with no check for overflow, though division by 0 is trapped and flagged as an error. The operators and their precedence, associativity, and values are the same as in the C language. The following list of operators is grouped into levels of equal-precedence operators. The levels are listed in order of decreasing precedence.

`id++ id--`   variable post-increment and post-decrement

`++id --id`   variable pre-increment and pre-decrement

`- +`   unary minus and plus

`! ~`   logical and bitwise negation

`**`   exponentiation

`* / %`   multiplication, division, remainder

`+ -`   addition, subtraction

`<< >>`   left and right bitwise shifts

`<= >= < >`   comparison

`== !=`   equality and inequality

&	bitwise AND
^	bitwise exclusive OR
|	bitwise OR
&&	logical AND
||	logical OR

`expr ? expr : expr`
> conditional operator

`= *= /= %= += -= <<= >>= &= ^= |=`
> assignment

`expr1 , expr2`
> comma

Shell variables are allowed as operands; parameter expansion is performed before the expression is evaluated. Within an expression, shell variables may also be referenced by name without using the parameter expansion syntax. A shell variable that is null or unset evaluates to 0 when referenced by name without using the parameter expansion syntax. The value of a variable is evaluated as an arithmetic expression when it is referenced, or when a variable which has been given the *integer* attribute using '`declare -i`' is assigned a value. A null value evaluates to 0. A shell variable need not have its *integer* attribute turned on to be used in an expression.

Constants with a leading 0 are interpreted as octal numbers. A leading '`0x`' or '`0X`' denotes hexadecimal. Otherwise, numbers take the form [*base#*]*n*, where the optional *base* is a decimal number between 2 and 64 representing the arithmetic base, and *n* is a number in that base. If *base#* is omitted, then base 10 is used. When specifying *n*, the digits greater than 9 are represented by the lowercase letters, the uppercase letters, '`@`', and '`_`', in that order. If *base* is less than or equal to 36, lowercase and uppercase letters may be used interchangeably to represent numbers between 10 and 35.

Operators are evaluated in order of precedence. Sub-expressions in parentheses are evaluated first and may override the precedence rules above.

6.6 Aliases

Aliases allow a string to be substituted for a word when it is used as the first word of a simple command. The shell maintains a list of aliases that may be set and unset with the **alias** and **unalias** builtin commands.

The first word of each simple command, if unquoted, is checked to see if it has an alias. If so, that word is replaced by the text of the alias. The characters '`/`', '`$`', '`` ` ``', '`=`' and any of the shell metacharacters or quoting characters listed above may not appear in an alias name. The replacement text may contain any valid shell input, including shell metacharacters. The first word of the replacement text is tested for aliases, but a word that is identical to an alias being expanded is not expanded a second time. This means that one may alias `ls` to `"ls -F"`, for instance, and Bash does not try to recursively expand the replacement text. If the last character of the alias value is a *blank*, then the next command word following the alias is also checked for alias expansion.

Aliases are created and listed with the **alias** command, and removed with the **unalias** command.

There is no mechanism for using arguments in the replacement text, as in **csh**. If arguments are needed, a shell function should be used (see Section 3.3 [Shell Functions], page 17).

Aliases are not expanded when the shell is not interactive, unless the **expand_aliases** shell option is set using **shopt** (see Section 4.3.2 [The Shopt Builtin], page 64).

The rules concerning the definition and use of aliases are somewhat confusing. Bash always reads at least one complete line of input before executing any of the commands on that line. Aliases are expanded when a command is read, not when it is executed. Therefore, an alias definition appearing on the same line as another command does not take effect until the next line of input is read. The commands following the alias definition on that line are not affected by the new alias. This behavior is also an issue when functions are executed. Aliases are expanded when a function definition is read, not when the function is executed, because a function definition is itself a command. As a consequence, aliases defined in a function are not available until after that function is executed. To be safe, always put alias definitions on a separate line, and do not use **alias** in compound commands.

For almost every purpose, shell functions are preferred over aliases.

6.7 Arrays

Bash provides one-dimensional indexed and associative array variables. Any variable may be used as an indexed array; the **declare** builtin will explicitly declare an array. There is no maximum limit on the size of an array, nor any requirement that members be indexed or assigned contiguously. Indexed arrays are referenced using integers (including arithmetic expressions (see Section 6.5 [Shell Arithmetic], page 89)) and are zero-based; associative arrays use arbitrary strings. Unless otherwise noted, indexed array indices must be non-negative integers.

An indexed array is created automatically if any variable is assigned to using the syntax

    name[subscript]=value

The *subscript* is treated as an arithmetic expression that must evaluate to a number. To explicitly declare an array, use

    declare -a name

The syntax

    declare -a name[subscript]

is also accepted; the *subscript* is ignored.

Associative arrays are created using

    declare -A name.

Attributes may be specified for an array variable using the **declare** and **readonly** builtins. Each attribute applies to all members of an array.

Arrays are assigned to using compound assignments of the form

    name=(value1 value2 ...)

where each *value* is of the form [*subscript*]=*string*. Indexed array assignments do not require anything but *string*. When assigning to indexed arrays, if the optional subscript is supplied, that index is assigned to; otherwise the index of the element assigned is the last index assigned to by the statement plus one. Indexing starts at zero.

When assigning to an associative array, the subscript is required.

This syntax is also accepted by the `declare` builtin. Individual array elements may be assigned to using the `name[subscript]=value` syntax introduced above.

When assigning to an indexed array, if *name* is subscripted by a negative number, that number is interpreted as relative to one greater than the maximum index of *name*, so negative indices count back from the end of the array, and an index of -1 references the last element.

Any element of an array may be referenced using `${name[subscript]}`. The braces are required to avoid conflicts with the shell's filename expansion operators. If the *subscript* is '@' or '*', the word expands to all members of the array *name*. These subscripts differ only when the word appears within double quotes. If the word is double-quoted, `${name[*]}` expands to a single word with the value of each array member separated by the first character of the `IFS` variable, and `${name[@]}` expands each element of *name* to a separate word. When there are no array members, `${name[@]}` expands to nothing. If the double-quoted expansion occurs within a word, the expansion of the first parameter is joined with the beginning part of the original word, and the expansion of the last parameter is joined with the last part of the original word. This is analogous to the expansion of the special parameters '@' and '*'. `${#name[subscript]}` expands to the length of `${name[subscript]}`. If *subscript* is '@' or '*', the expansion is the number of elements in the array. If the *subscript* used to reference an element of an indexed array evaluates to a number less than zero, it is interpreted as relative to one greater than the maximum index of the array, so negative indices count back from the end of the array, and an index of -1 refers to the last element.

Referencing an array variable without a subscript is equivalent to referencing with a subscript of 0. Any reference to a variable using a valid subscript is legal, and `bash` will create an array if necessary.

An array variable is considered set if a subscript has been assigned a value. The null string is a valid value.

It is possible to obtain the keys (indices) of an array as well as the values. ${!*name*[@]} and ${!*name*[*]} expand to the indices assigned in array variable *name*. The treatment when in double quotes is similar to the expansion of the special parameters '@' and '*' within double quotes.

The `unset` builtin is used to destroy arrays. `unset name[subscript]` destroys the array element at index *subscript*. Negative subscripts to indexed arrays are interpreted as described above. Care must be taken to avoid unwanted side effects caused by filename expansion. `unset name`, where *name* is an array, removes the entire array. A subscript of '*' or '@' also removes the entire array.

The `declare`, `local`, and `readonly` builtins each accept a `-a` option to specify an indexed array and a `-A` option to specify an associative array. If both options are supplied, `-A` takes precedence. The `read` builtin accepts a `-a` option to assign a list of words read from the standard input to an array, and can read values from the standard input into individual array elements. The `set` and `declare` builtins display array values in a way that allows them to be reused as input.

6.8 The Directory Stack

The directory stack is a list of recently-visited directories. The `pushd` builtin adds directories to the stack as it changes the current directory, and the `popd` builtin removes specified directories from the stack and changes the current directory to the directory removed. The `dirs` builtin displays the contents of the directory stack. The current directory is always the "top" of the directory stack.

The contents of the directory stack are also visible as the value of the `DIRSTACK` shell variable.

6.8.1 Directory Stack Builtins

`dirs`

> `dirs [-clpv] [+N | -N]`
>
> Display the list of currently remembered directories. Directories are added to the list with the `pushd` command; the `popd` command removes directories from the list. The current directory is always the first directory in the stack.
>
> | | |
> |---|---|
> | `-c` | Clears the directory stack by deleting all of the elements. |
> | `-l` | Produces a listing using full pathnames; the default listing format uses a tilde to denote the home directory. |
> | `-p` | Causes `dirs` to print the directory stack with one entry per line. |
> | `-v` | Causes `dirs` to print the directory stack with one entry per line, prefixing each entry with its index in the stack. |
> | `+N` | Displays the Nth directory (counting from the left of the list printed by `dirs` when invoked without options), starting with zero. |
> | `-N` | Displays the Nth directory (counting from the right of the list printed by `dirs` when invoked without options), starting with zero. |

`popd`

> `popd [-n] [+N | -N]`
>
> When no arguments are given, `popd` removes the top directory from the stack and performs a `cd` to the new top directory. The elements are numbered from 0 starting at the first directory listed with `dirs`; that is, `popd` is equivalent to `popd +0`.
>
> | | |
> |---|---|
> | `-n` | Suppresses the normal change of directory when removing directories from the stack, so that only the stack is manipulated. |
> | `+N` | Removes the Nth directory (counting from the left of the list printed by `dirs`), starting with zero. |
> | `-N` | Removes the Nth directory (counting from the right of the list printed by `dirs`), starting with zero. |

`pushd`

> `pushd [-n] [+N | -N | dir]`

Save the current directory on the top of the directory stack and then **cd** to *dir*. With no arguments, **pushd** exchanges the top two directories and makes the new top the current directory.

-n   Suppresses the normal change of directory when rotating or adding directories to the stack, so that only the stack is manipulated.

+*N*   Brings the *N*th directory (counting from the left of the list printed by **dirs**, starting with zero) to the top of the list by rotating the stack.

-*N*   Brings the *N*th directory (counting from the right of the list printed by **dirs**, starting with zero) to the top of the list by rotating the stack.

dir   Makes *dir* be the top of the stack, making it the new current directory as if it had been supplied as an argument to the **cd** builtin.

6.9 Controlling the Prompt

The value of the variable PROMPT_COMMAND is examined just before Bash prints each primary prompt. If PROMPT_COMMAND is set and has a non-null value, then the value is executed just as if it had been typed on the command line.

In addition, the following table describes the special characters which can appear in the prompt variables PS1 to PS4:

\a   A bell character.

\d   The date, in "Weekday Month Date" format (e.g., "Tue May 26").

\D{*format*}

     The *format* is passed to **strftime**(3) and the result is inserted into the prompt string; an empty *format* results in a locale-specific time representation. The braces are required.

\e   An escape character.

\h   The hostname, up to the first '.'.

\H   The hostname.

\j   The number of jobs currently managed by the shell.

\l   The basename of the shell's terminal device name.

\n   A newline.

\r   A carriage return.

\s   The name of the shell, the basename of $0 (the portion following the final slash).

\t   The time, in 24-hour HH:MM:SS format.

\T   The time, in 12-hour HH:MM:SS format.

\@   The time, in 12-hour am/pm format.

\A   The time, in 24-hour HH:MM format.

\u	The username of the current user.
\v	The version of Bash (e.g., 2.00)
\V	The release of Bash, version + patchlevel (e.g., 2.00.0)
\w	The current working directory, with $HOME abbreviated with a tilde (uses the $PROMPT_DIRTRIM variable).
\W	The basename of $PWD, with $HOME abbreviated with a tilde.
\!	The history number of this command.
\#	The command number of this command.
\$	If the effective uid is 0, #, otherwise $.
\nnn	The character whose ASCII code is the octal value nnn.
\\	A backslash.
\[	Begin a sequence of non-printing characters. This could be used to embed a terminal control sequence into the prompt.
\]	End a sequence of non-printing characters.

The command number and the history number are usually different: the history number of a command is its position in the history list, which may include commands restored from the history file (see Section 9.1 [Bash History Facilities], page 137), while the command number is the position in the sequence of commands executed during the current shell session.

After the string is decoded, it is expanded via parameter expansion, command substitution, arithmetic expansion, and quote removal, subject to the value of the promptvars shell option (see Section 4.2 [Bash Builtins], page 49).

6.10 The Restricted Shell

If Bash is started with the name rbash, or the --restricted or -r option is supplied at invocation, the shell becomes restricted. A restricted shell is used to set up an environment more controlled than the standard shell. A restricted shell behaves identically to bash with the exception that the following are disallowed or not performed:

- Changing directories with the cd builtin.
- Setting or unsetting the values of the SHELL, PATH, ENV, or BASH_ENV variables.
- Specifying command names containing slashes.
- Specifying a filename containing a slash as an argument to the . builtin command.
- Specifying a filename containing a slash as an argument to the -p option to the hash builtin command.
- Importing function definitions from the shell environment at startup.
- Parsing the value of SHELLOPTS from the shell environment at startup.
- Redirecting output using the '>', '>|', '<>', '>&', '&>', and '>>' redirection operators.
- Using the exec builtin to replace the shell with another command.
- Adding or deleting builtin commands with the -f and -d options to the enable builtin.

- Using the **enable** builtin command to enable disabled shell builtins.
- Specifying the -p option to the **command** builtin.
- Turning off restricted mode with 'set +r' or 'set +o restricted'.

These restrictions are enforced after any startup files are read.

When a command that is found to be a shell script is executed (see Section 3.8 [Shell Scripts], page 40), **rbash** turns off any restrictions in the shell spawned to execute the script.

6.11 Bash POSIX Mode

Starting Bash with the --posix command-line option or executing 'set -o posix' while Bash is running will cause Bash to conform more closely to the POSIX standard by changing the behavior to match that specified by POSIX in areas where the Bash default differs.

When invoked as **sh**, Bash enters POSIX mode after reading the startup files.

The following list is what's changed when 'POSIX mode' is in effect:

1. When a command in the hash table no longer exists, Bash will re-search $PATH to find the new location. This is also available with 'shopt -s checkhash'.

2. The message printed by the job control code and builtins when a job exits with a non-zero status is 'Done(status)'.

3. The message printed by the job control code and builtins when a job is stopped is 'Stopped(*signame*)', where *signame* is, for example, SIGTSTP.

4. Alias expansion is always enabled, even in non-interactive shells.

5. Reserved words appearing in a context where reserved words are recognized do not undergo alias expansion.

6. The POSIX PS1 and PS2 expansions of '!' to the history number and '!!' to '!' are enabled, and parameter expansion is performed on the values of PS1 and PS2 regardless of the setting of the **promptvars** option.

7. The POSIX startup files are executed ($ENV) rather than the normal Bash files.

8. Tilde expansion is only performed on assignments preceding a command name, rather than on all assignment statements on the line.

9. The default history file is ~/.sh_history (this is the default value of $HISTFILE).

10. Redirection operators do not perform filename expansion on the word in the redirection unless the shell is interactive.

11. Redirection operators do not perform word splitting on the word in the redirection.

12. Function names must be valid shell **names**. That is, they may not contain characters other than letters, digits, and underscores, and may not start with a digit. Declaring a function with an invalid name causes a fatal syntax error in non-interactive shells.

13. Function names may not be the same as one of the POSIX special builtins.

14. POSIX special builtins are found before shell functions during command lookup.

15. When printing shell function definitions (e.g., by **type**), Bash does not print the **function** keyword.

16. Literal tildes that appear as the first character in elements of the PATH variable are not expanded as described above under Section 3.5.2 [Tilde Expansion], page 22.

17. The `time` reserved word may be used by itself as a command. When used in this way, it displays timing statistics for the shell and its completed children. The `TIMEFORMAT` variable controls the format of the timing information.

18. When parsing and expanding a ${...} expansion that appears within double quotes, single quotes are no longer special and cannot be used to quote a closing brace or other special character, unless the operator is one of those defined to perform pattern removal. In this case, they do not have to appear as matched pairs.

19. The parser does not recognize `time` as a reserved word if the next token begins with a '-'.

20. The '!' character does not introduce history expansion within a double-quoted string, even if the `histexpand` option is enabled.

21. If a POSIX special builtin returns an error status, a non-interactive shell exits. The fatal errors are those listed in the POSIX standard, and include things like passing incorrect options, redirection errors, variable assignment errors for assignments preceding the command name, and so on.

22. A non-interactive shell exits with an error status if a variable assignment error occurs when no command name follows the assignment statements. A variable assignment error occurs, for example, when trying to assign a value to a readonly variable.

23. A non-interactive shell exits with an error status if a variable assignment error occurs in an assignment statement preceding a special builtin, but not with any other simple command.

24. A non-interactive shell exits with an error status if the iteration variable in a `for` statement or the selection variable in a `select` statement is a readonly variable.

25. Non-interactive shells exit if *filename* in . *filename* is not found.

26. Non-interactive shells exit if a syntax error in an arithmetic expansion results in an invalid expression.

27. Non-interactive shells exit if a parameter expansion error occurs.

28. Non-interactive shells exit if there is a syntax error in a script read with the . or `source` builtins, or in a string processed by the `eval` builtin.

29. Process substitution is not available.

30. While variable indirection is available, it may not be applied to the '#' and '?' special parameters.

31. When expanding the '*' special parameter in a pattern context where the expansion is double-quoted does not treat the `$*` as if it were double-quoted.

32. Assignment statements preceding POSIX special builtins persist in the shell environment after the builtin completes.

33. Assignment statements preceding shell function calls persist in the shell environment after the function returns, as if a POSIX special builtin command had been executed.

34. The `command` builtin does not prevent builtins that take assignment statements as arguments from expanding them as assignment statements; when not in POSIX mode, assignment builtins lose their assignment statement expansion properties when preceded by `command`.

35. The `bg` builtin uses the required format to describe each job placed in the background, which does not include an indication of whether the job is the current or previous job.

36. The output of 'kill -l' prints all the signal names on a single line, separated by spaces, without the 'SIG' prefix.

37. The kill builtin does not accept signal names with a 'SIG' prefix.

38. The export and readonly builtin commands display their output in the format required by POSIX.

39. The trap builtin displays signal names without the leading SIG.

40. The trap builtin doesn't check the first argument for a possible signal specification and revert the signal handling to the original disposition if it is, unless that argument consists solely of digits and is a valid signal number. If users want to reset the handler for a given signal to the original disposition, they should use '-' as the first argument.

41. The . and source builtins do not search the current directory for the filename argument if it is not found by searching PATH.

42. Enabling POSIX mode has the effect of setting the inherit_errexit option, so subshells spawned to execute command substitutions inherit the value of the -e option from the parent shell. When the inherit_errexit option is not enabled, Bash clears the -e option in such subshells.

43. When the alias builtin displays alias definitions, it does not display them with a leading 'alias ' unless the -p option is supplied.

44. When the set builtin is invoked without options, it does not display shell function names and definitions.

45. When the set builtin is invoked without options, it displays variable values without quotes, unless they contain shell metacharacters, even if the result contains nonprinting characters.

46. When the cd builtin is invoked in *logical* mode, and the pathname constructed from $PWD and the directory name supplied as an argument does not refer to an existing directory, cd will fail instead of falling back to *physical* mode.

47. The pwd builtin verifies that the value it prints is the same as the current directory, even if it is not asked to check the file system with the -P option.

48. When listing the history, the fc builtin does not include an indication of whether or not a history entry has been modified.

49. The default editor used by fc is ed.

50. The type and command builtins will not report a non-executable file as having been found, though the shell will attempt to execute such a file if it is the only so-named file found in $PATH.

51. The vi editing mode will invoke the vi editor directly when the 'v' command is run, instead of checking $VISUAL and $EDITOR.

52. When the xpg_echo option is enabled, Bash does not attempt to interpret any arguments to echo as options. Each argument is displayed, after escape characters are converted.

53. The ulimit builtin uses a block size of 512 bytes for the -c and -f options.

54. The arrival of SIGCHLD when a trap is set on SIGCHLD does not interrupt the wait builtin and cause it to return immediately. The trap command is run once for each child that exits.

55. The `read` builtin may be interrupted by a signal for which a trap has been set. If Bash receives a trapped signal while executing `read`, the trap handler executes and `read` returns an exit status greater than 128.

56. Bash removes an exited background process's status from the list of such statuses after the `wait` builtin is used to obtain it.

There is other POSIX behavior that Bash does not implement by default even when in POSIX mode. Specifically:

1. The `fc` builtin checks `$EDITOR` as a program to edit history entries if FCEDIT is unset, rather than defaulting directly to `ed`. `fc` uses `ed` if EDITOR is unset.

2. As noted above, Bash requires the `xpg_echo` option to be enabled for the `echo` builtin to be fully conformant.

Bash can be configured to be POSIX-conformant by default, by specifying the `--enable-strict-posix-default` to `configure` when building (see Section 10.8 [Optional Features], page 144).

7 Job Control

This chapter discusses what job control is, how it works, and how Bash allows you to access its facilities.

7.1 Job Control Basics

Job control refers to the ability to selectively stop (suspend) the execution of processes and continue (resume) their execution at a later point. A user typically employs this facility via an interactive interface supplied jointly by the operating system kernel's terminal driver and Bash.

The shell associates a *job* with each pipeline. It keeps a table of currently executing jobs, which may be listed with the `jobs` command. When Bash starts a job asynchronously, it prints a line that looks like:

    [1] 25647

indicating that this job is job number 1 and that the process ID of the last process in the pipeline associated with this job is 25647. All of the processes in a single pipeline are members of the same job. Bash uses the *job* abstraction as the basis for job control.

To facilitate the implementation of the user interface to job control, the operating system maintains the notion of a current terminal process group ID. Members of this process group (processes whose process group ID is equal to the current terminal process group ID) receive keyboard-generated signals such as `SIGINT`. These processes are said to be in the foreground. Background processes are those whose process group ID differs from the terminal's; such processes are immune to keyboard-generated signals. Only foreground processes are allowed to read from or, if the user so specifies with `stty tostop`, write to the terminal. Background processes which attempt to read from (write to when `stty tostop` is in effect) the terminal are sent a `SIGTTIN` (`SIGTTOU`) signal by the kernel's terminal driver, which, unless caught, suspends the process.

If the operating system on which Bash is running supports job control, Bash contains facilities to use it. Typing the *suspend* character (typically '^Z', Control-Z) while a process is running causes that process to be stopped and returns control to Bash. Typing the *delayed suspend* character (typically '^Y', Control-Y) causes the process to be stopped when it attempts to read input from the terminal, and control to be returned to Bash. The user then manipulates the state of this job, using the `bg` command to continue it in the background, the `fg` command to continue it in the foreground, or the `kill` command to kill it. A '^Z' takes effect immediately, and has the additional side effect of causing pending output and typeahead to be discarded.

There are a number of ways to refer to a job in the shell. The character '%' introduces a job specification (*jobspec*).

Job number n may be referred to as '%n'. The symbols '%%' and '%+' refer to the shell's notion of the current job, which is the last job stopped while it was in the foreground or started in the background. A single '%' (with no accompanying job specification) also refers to the current job. The previous job may be referenced using '%-'. If there is only a single job, '%+' and '%-' can both be used to refer to that job. In output pertaining to jobs (e.g., the output of the `jobs` command), the current job is always flagged with a '+', and the previous job with a '-'.

A job may also be referred to using a prefix of the name used to start it, or using a substring that appears in its command line. For example, '%ce' refers to a stopped ce job. Using '%?ce', on the other hand, refers to any job containing the string 'ce' in its command line. If the prefix or substring matches more than one job, Bash reports an error.

Simply naming a job can be used to bring it into the foreground: '%1' is a synonym for 'fg %1', bringing job 1 from the background into the foreground. Similarly, '%1 &' resumes job 1 in the background, equivalent to 'bg %1'

The shell learns immediately whenever a job changes state. Normally, Bash waits until it is about to print a prompt before reporting changes in a job's status so as to not interrupt any other output. If the -b option to the set builtin is enabled, Bash reports such changes immediately (see Section 4.3.1 [The Set Builtin], page 60). Any trap on SIGCHLD is executed for each child process that exits.

If an attempt to exit Bash is made while jobs are stopped, (or running, if the checkjobs option is enabled – see Section 4.3.2 [The Shopt Builtin], page 64), the shell prints a warning message, and if the checkjobs option is enabled, lists the jobs and their statuses. The jobs command may then be used to inspect their status. If a second attempt to exit is made without an intervening command, Bash does not print another warning, and any stopped jobs are terminated.

7.2 Job Control Builtins

bg

        bg [*jobspec* ...]

        Resume each suspended job *jobspec* in the background, as if it had been started with '&'. If *jobspec* is not supplied, the current job is used. The return status is zero unless it is run when job control is not enabled, or, when run with job control enabled, any *jobspec* was not found or specifies a job that was started without job control.

fg

        fg [*jobspec*]

        Resume the job *jobspec* in the foreground and make it the current job. If *jobspec* is not supplied, the current job is used. The return status is that of the command placed into the foreground, or non-zero if run when job control is disabled or, when run with job control enabled, *jobspec* does not specify a valid job or *jobspec* specifies a job that was started without job control.

jobs

        jobs [-lnprs] [*jobspec*]
        jobs -x *command* [*arguments*]

        The first form lists the active jobs. The options have the following meanings:

        -l   List process IDs in addition to the normal information.

        -n   Display information only about jobs that have changed status since the user was last notified of their status.

        -p   List only the process ID of the job's process group leader.

-r   Display only running jobs.

-s   Display only stopped jobs.

If *jobspec* is given, output is restricted to information about that job. If *jobspec* is not supplied, the status of all jobs is listed.

If the -x option is supplied, `jobs` replaces any *jobspec* found in *command* or *arguments* with the corresponding process group ID, and executes *command*, passing it *arguments*, returning its exit status.

kill

```
kill [-s sigspec] [-n signum] [-sigspec] jobspec or pid
kill -l|-L [exit_status]
```

Send a signal specified by *sigspec* or *signum* to the process named by job specification *jobspec* or process ID *pid*. *sigspec* is either a case-insensitive signal name such as SIGINT (with or without the SIG prefix) or a signal number; *signum* is a signal number. If *sigspec* and *signum* are not present, SIGTERM is used. The -l option lists the signal names. If any arguments are supplied when -l is given, the names of the signals corresponding to the arguments are listed, and the return status is zero. *exit_status* is a number specifying a signal number or the exit status of a process terminated by a signal. The -L option is equivalent to -l. The return status is zero if at least one signal was successfully sent, or non-zero if an error occurs or an invalid option is encountered.

wait

```
wait [-n] [jobspec or pid ...]
```

Wait until the child process specified by each process ID *pid* or job specification *jobspec* exits and return the exit status of the last command waited for. If a job spec is given, all processes in the job are waited for. If no arguments are given, all currently active child processes are waited for, and the return status is zero. If the -n option is supplied, `wait` waits for any job to terminate and returns its exit status. If neither *jobspec* nor *pid* specifies an active child process of the shell, the return status is 127.

disown

```
disown [-ar] [-h] [jobspec ... | pid ... ]
```

Without options, remove each *jobspec* from the table of active jobs. If the -h option is given, the job is not removed from the table, but is marked so that SIGHUP is not sent to the job if the shell receives a SIGHUP. If *jobspec* is not present, and neither the -a nor the -r option is supplied, the current job is used. If no *jobspec* is supplied, the -a option means to remove or mark all jobs; the -r option without a *jobspec* argument restricts operation to running jobs.

suspend

```
suspend [-f]
```

Suspend the execution of this shell until it receives a SIGCONT signal. A login shell cannot be suspended; the -f option can be used to override this and force the suspension.

When job control is not active, the `kill` and `wait` builtins do not accept *jobspec* arguments. They must be supplied process IDs.

7.3 Job Control Variables

`auto_resume`

This variable controls how the shell interacts with the user and job control. If this variable exists then single word simple commands without redirections are treated as candidates for resumption of an existing job. There is no ambiguity allowed; if there is more than one job beginning with the string typed, then the most recently accessed job will be selected. The name of a stopped job, in this context, is the command line used to start it. If this variable is set to the value 'exact', the string supplied must match the name of a stopped job exactly; if set to 'substring', the string supplied needs to match a substring of the name of a stopped job. The 'substring' value provides functionality analogous to the '%?' job ID (see Section 7.1 [Job Control Basics], page 100). If set to any other value, the supplied string must be a prefix of a stopped job's name; this provides functionality analogous to the '%' job ID.

8 Command Line Editing

This chapter describes the basic features of the GNU command line editing interface. Command line editing is provided by the Readline library, which is used by several different programs, including Bash. Command line editing is enabled by default when using an interactive shell, unless the --noediting option is supplied at shell invocation. Line editing is also used when using the -e option to the read builtin command (see Section 4.2 [Bash Builtins], page 49). By default, the line editing commands are similar to those of Emacs. A vi-style line editing interface is also available. Line editing can be enabled at any time using the -o emacs or -o vi options to the set builtin command (see Section 4.3.1 [The Set Builtin], page 60), or disabled using the +o emacs or +o vi options to set.

8.1 Introduction to Line Editing

The following paragraphs describe the notation used to represent keystrokes.

The text *C-k* is read as 'Control-K' and describes the character produced when the k key is pressed while the Control key is depressed.

The text *M-k* is read as 'Meta-K' and describes the character produced when the Meta key (if you have one) is depressed, and the k key is pressed. The Meta key is labeled ALT on many keyboards. On keyboards with two keys labeled ALT (usually to either side of the space bar), the ALT on the left side is generally set to work as a Meta key. The ALT key on the right may also be configured to work as a Meta key or may be configured as some other modifier, such as a Compose key for typing accented characters.

If you do not have a Meta or ALT key, or another key working as a Meta key, the identical keystroke can be generated by typing ESC *first*, and then typing k. Either process is known as *metafying* the k key.

The text *M-C-k* is read as 'Meta-Control-k' and describes the character produced by *metafying* *C-k*.

In addition, several keys have their own names. Specifically, DEL, ESC, LFD, SPC, RET, and TAB all stand for themselves when seen in this text, or in an init file (see Section 8.3 [Readline Init File], page 107). If your keyboard lacks a LFD key, typing C-j will produce the desired character. The RET key may be labeled Return or Enter on some keyboards.

8.2 Readline Interaction

Often during an interactive session you type in a long line of text, only to notice that the first word on the line is misspelled. The Readline library gives you a set of commands for manipulating the text as you type it in, allowing you to just fix your typo, and not forcing you to retype the majority of the line. Using these editing commands, you move the cursor to the place that needs correction, and delete or insert the text of the corrections. Then, when you are satisfied with the line, you simply press RET. You do not have to be at the end of the line to press RET; the entire line is accepted regardless of the location of the cursor within the line.

8.2.1 Readline Bare Essentials

In order to enter characters into the line, simply type them. The typed character appears where the cursor was, and then the cursor moves one space to the right. If you mistype a character, you can use your erase character to back up and delete the mistyped character.

Sometimes you may mistype a character, and not notice the error until you have typed several other characters. In that case, you can type *C-b* to move the cursor to the left, and then correct your mistake. Afterwards, you can move the cursor to the right with *C-f*.

When you add text in the middle of a line, you will notice that characters to the right of the cursor are 'pushed over' to make room for the text that you have inserted. Likewise, when you delete text behind the cursor, characters to the right of the cursor are 'pulled back' to fill in the blank space created by the removal of the text. A list of the bare essentials for editing the text of an input line follows.

C-b   Move back one character.

C-f   Move forward one character.

DEL or Backspace
            Delete the character to the left of the cursor.

C-d   Delete the character underneath the cursor.

Printing characters
            Insert the character into the line at the cursor.

C-_ or *C-x C-u*
            Undo the last editing command. You can undo all the way back to an empty line.

(Depending on your configuration, the Backspace key be set to delete the character to the left of the cursor and the DEL key set to delete the character underneath the cursor, like *C-d*, rather than the character to the left of the cursor.)

8.2.2 Readline Movement Commands

The above table describes the most basic keystrokes that you need in order to do editing of the input line. For your convenience, many other commands have been added in addition to *C-b*, *C-f*, *C-d*, and DEL. Here are some commands for moving more rapidly about the line.

C-a   Move to the start of the line.

C-e   Move to the end of the line.

M-f   Move forward a word, where a word is composed of letters and digits.

M-b   Move backward a word.

C-l   Clear the screen, reprinting the current line at the top.

Notice how *C-f* moves forward a character, while *M-f* moves forward a word. It is a loose convention that control keystrokes operate on characters while meta keystrokes operate on words.

8.2.3 Readline Killing Commands

Killing text means to delete the text from the line, but to save it away for later use, usually by *yanking* (re-inserting) it back into the line. ('Cut' and 'paste' are more recent jargon for 'kill' and 'yank'.)

If the description for a command says that it 'kills' text, then you can be sure that you can get the text back in a different (or the same) place later.

When you use a kill command, the text is saved in a *kill-ring*. Any number of consecutive kills save all of the killed text together, so that when you yank it back, you get it all. The kill ring is not line specific; the text that you killed on a previously typed line is available to be yanked back later, when you are typing another line.

Here is the list of commands for killing text.

C-k   Kill the text from the current cursor position to the end of the line.

M-d   Kill from the cursor to the end of the current word, or, if between words, to the end of the next word. Word boundaries are the same as those used by *M-f*.

M-DEL   Kill from the cursor the start of the current word, or, if between words, to the start of the previous word. Word boundaries are the same as those used by *M-b*.

C-w   Kill from the cursor to the previous whitespace. This is different than *M-DEL* because the word boundaries differ.

Here is how to *yank* the text back into the line. Yanking means to copy the most-recently-killed text from the kill buffer.

C-y   Yank the most recently killed text back into the buffer at the cursor.

M-y   Rotate the kill-ring, and yank the new top. You can only do this if the prior command is *C-y* or *M-y*.

8.2.4 Readline Arguments

You can pass numeric arguments to Readline commands. Sometimes the argument acts as a repeat count, other times it is the *sign* of the argument that is significant. If you pass a negative argument to a command which normally acts in a forward direction, that command will act in a backward direction. For example, to kill text back to the start of the line, you might type 'M-- C-k'.

The general way to pass numeric arguments to a command is to type meta digits before the command. If the first 'digit' typed is a minus sign ('-'), then the sign of the argument will be negative. Once you have typed one meta digit to get the argument started, you can type the remainder of the digits, and then the command. For example, to give the *C-d* command an argument of 10, you could type 'M-1 0 C-d', which will delete the next ten characters on the input line.

8.2.5 Searching for Commands in the History

Readline provides commands for searching through the command history (see Section 9.1 [Bash History Facilities], page 137) for lines containing a specified string. There are two search modes: *incremental* and *non-incremental*.

Incremental searches begin before the user has finished typing the search string. As each character of the search string is typed, Readline displays the next entry from the history matching the string typed so far. An incremental search requires only as many characters as needed to find the desired history entry. To search backward in the history for a particular string, type *C-r*. Typing *C-s* searches forward through the history. The characters present in the value of the `isearch-terminators` variable are used to terminate an incremental search. If that variable has not been assigned a value, the ESC and *C-J* characters will terminate an incremental search. *C-g* will abort an incremental search and restore the original line. When the search is terminated, the history entry containing the search string becomes the current line.

To find other matching entries in the history list, type *C-r* or *C-s* as appropriate. This will search backward or forward in the history for the next entry matching the search string typed so far. Any other key sequence bound to a Readline command will terminate the search and execute that command. For instance, a RET will terminate the search and accept the line, thereby executing the command from the history list. A movement command will terminate the search, make the last line found the current line, and begin editing.

Readline remembers the last incremental search string. If two *C-r*s are typed without any intervening characters defining a new search string, any remembered search string is used.

Non-incremental searches read the entire search string before starting to search for matching history lines. The search string may be typed by the user or be part of the contents of the current line.

8.3 Readline Init File

Although the Readline library comes with a set of Emacs-like keybindings installed by default, it is possible to use a different set of keybindings. Any user can customize programs that use Readline by putting commands in an *inputrc* file, conventionally in his home directory. The name of this file is taken from the value of the shell variable INPUTRC. If that variable is unset, the default is `~/.inputrc`. If that file does not exist or cannot be read, the ultimate default is `/etc/inputrc`.

When a program which uses the Readline library starts up, the init file is read, and the key bindings are set.

In addition, the `C-x C-r` command re-reads this init file, thus incorporating any changes that you might have made to it.

8.3.1 Readline Init File Syntax

There are only a few basic constructs allowed in the Readline init file. Blank lines are ignored. Lines beginning with a '#' are comments. Lines beginning with a '$' indicate conditional constructs (see Section 8.3.2 [Conditional Init Constructs], page 115). Other lines denote variable settings and key bindings.

Variable Settings
> You can modify the run-time behavior of Readline by altering the values of variables in Readline using the `set` command within the init file. The syntax is simple:

> ```
> set variable value
> ```

Here, for example, is how to change from the default Emacs-like key binding to use `vi` line editing commands:

```
set editing-mode vi
```

Variable names and values, where appropriate, are recognized without regard to case. Unrecognized variable names are ignored.

Boolean variables (those that can be set to on or off) are set to on if the value is null or empty, *on* (case-insensitive), or 1. Any other value results in the variable being set to off.

The `bind -V` command lists the current Readline variable names and values. See Section 4.2 [Bash Builtins], page 49.

A great deal of run-time behavior is changeable with the following variables.

`bell-style`

> Controls what happens when Readline wants to ring the terminal bell. If set to 'none', Readline never rings the bell. If set to 'visible', Readline uses a visible bell if one is available. If set to 'audible' (the default), Readline attempts to ring the terminal's bell.

`bind-tty-special-chars`

> If set to 'on' (the default), Readline attempts to bind the control characters treated specially by the kernel's terminal driver to their Readline equivalents.

`blink-matching-paren`

> If set to 'on', Readline attempts to briefly move the cursor to an opening parenthesis when a closing parenthesis is inserted. The default is 'off'.

`colored-completion-prefix`

> If set to 'on', when listing completions, Readline displays the common prefix of the set of possible completions using a different color. The color definitions are taken from the value of the `LS_COLORS` environment variable. The default is 'off'.

`colored-stats`

> If set to 'on', Readline displays possible completions using different colors to indicate their file type. The color definitions are taken from the value of the `LS_COLORS` environment variable. The default is 'off'.

`comment-begin`

> The string to insert at the beginning of the line when the `insert-comment` command is executed. The default value is `"#"`.

`completion-display-width`

> The number of screen columns used to display possible matches when performing completion. The value is ignored if it is less than 0 or greater than the terminal screen width. A value of 0 will cause matches to be displayed one per line. The default value is -1.

completion-ignore-case

> If set to 'on', Readline performs filename matching and completion in a case-insensitive fashion. The default value is 'off'.

completion-map-case

> If set to 'on', and *completion-ignore-case* is enabled, Readline treats hyphens ('-') and underscores ('_') as equivalent when performing case-insensitive filename matching and completion.

completion-prefix-display-length

> The length in characters of the common prefix of a list of possible completions that is displayed without modification. When set to a value greater than zero, common prefixes longer than this value are replaced with an ellipsis when displaying possible completions.

completion-query-items

> The number of possible completions that determines when the user is asked whether the list of possibilities should be displayed. If the number of possible completions is greater than this value, Readline will ask the user whether or not he wishes to view them; otherwise, they are simply listed. This variable must be set to an integer value greater than or equal to 0. A negative value means Readline should never ask. The default limit is 100.

convert-meta

> If set to 'on', Readline will convert characters with the eighth bit set to an ASCII key sequence by stripping the eighth bit and prefixing an ESC character, converting them to a meta-prefixed key sequence. The default value is 'on', but will be set to 'off' if the locale is one that contains eight-bit characters.

disable-completion

> If set to 'On', Readline will inhibit word completion. Completion characters will be inserted into the line as if they had been mapped to **self-insert**. The default is 'off'.

echo-control-characters

> When set to 'on', on operating systems that indicate they support it, readline echoes a character corresponding to a signal generated from the keyboard. The default is 'on'.

editing-mode

> The **editing-mode** variable controls which default set of key bindings is used. By default, Readline starts up in Emacs editing mode, where the keystrokes are most similar to Emacs. This variable can be set to either 'emacs' or 'vi'.

emacs-mode-string

> This string is displayed immediately before the last line of the primary prompt when emacs editing mode is active. The value is expanded like a key binding, so the standard set of meta- and control prefixes and backslash escape sequences is available. Use the

'\1' and '\2' escapes to begin and end sequences of non-printing characters, which can be used to embed a terminal control sequence into the mode string. The default is '@'.

`enable-bracketed-paste`
When set to 'On', Readline will configure the terminal in a way that will enable it to insert each paste into the editing buffer as a single string of characters, instead of treating each character as if it had been read from the keyboard. This can prevent pasted characters from being interpreted as editing commands. The default is 'off'.

`enable-keypad`
When set to 'on', Readline will try to enable the application keypad when it is called. Some systems need this to enable the arrow keys. The default is 'off'.

`enable-meta-key`
When set to 'on', Readline will try to enable any meta modifier key the terminal claims to support when it is called. On many terminals, the meta key is used to send eight-bit characters. The default is 'on'.

`expand-tilde`
If set to 'on', tilde expansion is performed when Readline attempts word completion. The default is 'off'.

`history-preserve-point`
If set to 'on', the history code attempts to place the point (the current cursor position) at the same location on each history line retrieved with **previous-history** or **next-history**. The default is 'off'.

`history-size`
Set the maximum number of history entries saved in the history list. If set to zero, any existing history entries are deleted and no new entries are saved. If set to a value less than zero, the number of history entries is not limited. By default, the number of history entries is not limited. If an attempt is made to set *history-size* to a non-numeric value, the maximum number of history entries will be set to 500.

`horizontal-scroll-mode`
This variable can be set to either 'on' or 'off'. Setting it to 'on' means that the text of the lines being edited will scroll horizontally on a single screen line when they are longer than the width of the screen, instead of wrapping onto a new screen line. By default, this variable is set to 'off'.

`input-meta`
If set to 'on', Readline will enable eight-bit input (it will not clear the eighth bit in the characters it reads), regardless of what the

terminal claims it can support. The default value is 'off', but Readline will set it to 'on' if the locale contains eight-bit characters. The name `meta-flag` is a synonym for this variable.

`isearch-terminators`

The string of characters that should terminate an incremental search without subsequently executing the character as a command (see Section 8.2.5 [Searching], page 106). If this variable has not been given a value, the characters ESC and *C-J* will terminate an incremental search.

`keymap`   Sets Readline's idea of the current keymap for key binding commands. Acceptable `keymap` names are `emacs`, `emacs-standard`, `emacs-meta`, `emacs-ctlx`, `vi`, `vi-move`, `vi-command`, and `vi-insert`. `vi` is equivalent to `vi-command` (`vi-move` is also a synonym); `emacs` is equivalent to `emacs-standard`. The default value is `emacs`. The value of the `editing-mode` variable also affects the default keymap.

`keyseq-timeout`

Specifies the duration Readline will wait for a character when reading an ambiguous key sequence (one that can form a complete key sequence using the input read so far, or can take additional input to complete a longer key sequence). If no input is received within the timeout, Readline will use the shorter but complete key sequence. Readline uses this value to determine whether or not input is available on the current input source (`rl_instream` by default). The value is specified in milliseconds, so a value of 1000 means that Readline will wait one second for additional input. If this variable is set to a value less than or equal to zero, or to a non-numeric value, Readline will wait until another key is pressed to decide which key sequence to complete. The default value is `500`.

`mark-directories`

If set to 'on', completed directory names have a slash appended. The default is 'on'.

`mark-modified-lines`

This variable, when set to 'on', causes Readline to display an asterisk ('*') at the start of history lines which have been modified. This variable is 'off' by default.

`mark-symlinked-directories`

If set to 'on', completed names which are symbolic links to directories have a slash appended (subject to the value of `mark-directories`). The default is 'off'.

`match-hidden-files`

This variable, when set to 'on', causes Readline to match files whose names begin with a '.' (hidden files) when performing filename completion. If set to 'off', the leading '.' must be supplied by the user in the filename to be completed. This variable is 'on' by default.

`menu-complete-display-prefix`

If set to 'on', menu completion displays the common prefix of the list of possible completions (which may be empty) before cycling through the list. The default is 'off'.

`output-meta`

If set to 'on', Readline will display characters with the eighth bit set directly rather than as a meta-prefixed escape sequence. The default is 'off', but Readline will set it to 'on' if the locale contains eight-bit characters.

`page-completions`

If set to 'on', Readline uses an internal `more`-like pager to display a screenful of possible completions at a time. This variable is 'on' by default.

`print-completions-horizontally`

If set to 'on', Readline will display completions with matches sorted horizontally in alphabetical order, rather than down the screen. The default is 'off'.

`revert-all-at-newline`

If set to 'on', Readline will undo all changes to history lines before returning when `accept-line` is executed. By default, history lines may be modified and retain individual undo lists across calls to `readline`. The default is 'off'.

`show-all-if-ambiguous`

This alters the default behavior of the completion functions. If set to 'on', words which have more than one possible completion cause the matches to be listed immediately instead of ringing the bell. The default value is 'off'.

`show-all-if-unmodified`

This alters the default behavior of the completion functions in a fashion similar to *show-all-if-ambiguous*. If set to 'on', words which have more than one possible completion without any possible partial completion (the possible completions don't share a common prefix) cause the matches to be listed immediately instead of ringing the bell. The default value is 'off'.

`show-mode-in-prompt`

If set to 'on', add a character to the beginning of the prompt indicating the editing mode: emacs, vi command, or vi insertion. The mode strings are user-settable. The default value is 'off'.

`skip-completed-text`

If set to 'on', this alters the default completion behavior when inserting a single match into the line. It's only active when performing completion in the middle of a word. If enabled, readline does not insert characters from the completion that match characters after point in the word being completed, so portions of the word following the cursor are not duplicated. For instance, if this is enabled, attempting completion when the cursor is after the 'e' in 'Makefile' will result in 'Makefile' rather than 'Makefilefile', assuming there is a single possible completion. The default value is 'off'.

`vi-cmd-mode-string`

This string is displayed immediately before the last line of the primary prompt when vi editing mode is active and in command mode. The value is expanded like a key binding, so the standard set of meta- and control prefixes and backslash escape sequences is available. Use the '\1' and '\2' escapes to begin and end sequences of non-printing characters, which can be used to embed a terminal control sequence into the mode string. The default is '(cmd)'.

`vi-ins-mode-string`

This string is displayed immediately before the last line of the primary prompt when vi editing mode is active and in insertion mode. The value is expanded like a key binding, so the standard set of meta- and control prefixes and backslash escape sequences is available. Use the '\1' and '\2' escapes to begin and end sequences of non-printing characters, which can be used to embed a terminal control sequence into the mode string. The default is '(ins)'.

`visible-stats`

If set to 'on', a character denoting a file's type is appended to the filename when listing possible completions. The default is 'off'.

Key Bindings

The syntax for controlling key bindings in the init file is simple. First you need to find the name of the command that you want to change. The following sections contain tables of the command name, the default keybinding, if any, and a short description of what the command does.

Once you know the name of the command, simply place on a line in the init file the name of the key you wish to bind the command to, a colon, and then the name of the command. There can be no space between the key name and the colon – that will be interpreted as part of the key name. The name of the key can be expressed in different ways, depending on what you find most comfortable.

In addition to command names, readline allows keys to be bound to a string that is inserted when the key is pressed (a *macro*).

The `bind -p` command displays Readline function names and bindings in a format that can put directly into an initialization file. See Section 4.2 [Bash Builtins], page 49.

keyname: *function-name* or *macro*

keyname is the name of a key spelled out in English. For example:

```
Control-u: universal-argument
Meta-Rubout: backward-kill-word
Control-o: "> output"
```

In the above example, *C-u* is bound to the function
universal-argument, *M-DEL* is bound to the function
backward-kill-word, and *C-o* is bound to run the macro
expressed on the right hand side (that is, to insert the text '>
output' into the line).

A number of symbolic character names are recognized while
processing this key binding syntax: *DEL*, *ESC*, *ESCAPE*, *LFD*,
NEWLINE, *RET*, *RETURN*, *RUBOUT*, *SPACE*, *SPC*, and *TAB*.

"*keyseq*": *function-name* or *macro*

> *keyseq* differs from *keyname* above in that strings denoting an en-
> tire key sequence can be specified, by placing the key sequence in
> double quotes. Some GNU Emacs style key escapes can be used, as
> in the following example, but the special character names are not
> recognized.

```
"\C-u": universal-argument
"\C-x\C-r": re-read-init-file
"\e[11~": "Function Key 1"
```

In the above example, *C-u* is again bound to the function
universal-argument (just as it was in the first example), '*C-x
C-r*' is bound to the function **re-read-init-file**, and 'ESC [1 1
~' is bound to insert the text 'Function Key 1'.

The following GNU Emacs style escape sequences are available when specifying
key sequences:

\C-	control prefix
\M-	meta prefix
\e	an escape character
\\	backslash
\"	", a double quotation mark
\'	', a single quote or apostrophe

In addition to the GNU Emacs style escape sequences, a second set of backslash
escapes is available:

\a	alert (bell)
\b	backspace
\d	delete
\f	form feed
\n	newline
\r	carriage return

`\t`	horizontal tab
`\v`	vertical tab
`\`*nnn*	the eight-bit character whose value is the octal value *nnn* (one to three digits)
`\x`*HH*	the eight-bit character whose value is the hexadecimal value *HH* (one or two hex digits)

When entering the text of a macro, single or double quotes must be used to indicate a macro definition. Unquoted text is assumed to be a function name. In the macro body, the backslash escapes described above are expanded. Backslash will quote any other character in the macro text, including '"' and '''. For example, the following binding will make '`C-x \`' insert a single '\' into the line:

```
"\C-x\\": "\\"
```

8.3.2 Conditional Init Constructs

Readline implements a facility similar in spirit to the conditional compilation features of the C preprocessor which allows key bindings and variable settings to be performed as the result of tests. There are four parser directives used.

`$if`   The `$if` construct allows bindings to be made based on the editing mode, the terminal being used, or the application using Readline. The text of the test extends to the end of the line; no characters are required to isolate it.

mode   The `mode=` form of the `$if` directive is used to test whether Readline is in `emacs` or `vi` mode. This may be used in conjunction with the 'set keymap' command, for instance, to set bindings in the `emacs-standard` and `emacs-ctlx` keymaps only if Readline is starting out in `emacs` mode.

term   The `term=` form may be used to include terminal-specific key bindings, perhaps to bind the key sequences output by the terminal's function keys. The word on the right side of the '=' is tested against both the full name of the terminal and the portion of the terminal name before the first '-'. This allows `sun` to match both `sun` and `sun-cmd`, for instance.

application

The *application* construct is used to include application-specific settings. Each program using the Readline library sets the *application name*, and you can test for a particular value. This could be used to bind key sequences to functions useful for a specific program. For instance, the following command adds a key sequence that quotes the current or previous word in Bash:

```
$if Bash
# Quote the current or previous word
"\C-xq": "\eb\"\ef\""
$endif
```

`$endif`   This command, as seen in the previous example, terminates an `$if` command.

$else   Commands in this branch of the $if directive are executed if the test fails.

$include   This directive takes a single filename as an argument and reads commands
            and bindings from that file. For example, the following directive reads from
            /etc/inputrc:

        $include /etc/inputrc

8.3.3 Sample Init File

Here is an example of an *inputrc* file. This illustrates key binding, variable assignment, and
conditional syntax.

```
# This file controls the behaviour of line input editing for
# programs that use the GNU Readline library.  Existing
# programs include FTP, Bash, and GDB.
#
# You can re-read the inputrc file with C-x C-r.
# Lines beginning with '#' are comments.
#
# First, include any system-wide bindings and variable
# assignments from /etc/Inputrc
$include /etc/Inputrc


#
# Set various bindings for emacs mode.

set editing-mode emacs

$if mode=emacs

Meta-Control-h:  backward-kill-word Text after the function name is ignored

#
# Arrow keys in keypad mode
#
#"\M-OD":        backward-char
#"\M-OC":        forward-char
#"\M-OA":        previous-history
#"\M-OB":        next-history
#
# Arrow keys in ANSI mode
#
"\M-[D":        backward-char
"\M-[C":        forward-char
"\M-[A":        previous-history
"\M-[B":        next-history
#
# Arrow keys in 8 bit keypad mode
#
#"\M-\C-OD":        backward-char
#"\M-\C-OC":        forward-char
#"\M-\C-OA":        previous-history
#"\M-\C-OB":        next-history
#
# Arrow keys in 8 bit ANSI mode
#
#"\M-\C-[D":        backward-char
#"\M-\C-[C":        forward-char
```

```
#"\M-\C-[A":        previous-history
#"\M-\C-[B":        next-history

C-q: quoted-insert

$endif

# An old-style binding.  This happens to be the default.
TAB: complete

# Macros that are convenient for shell interaction
$if Bash
# edit the path
"\C-xp": "PATH=${PATH}\e\C-e\C-a\ef\C-f"
# prepare to type a quoted word --
# insert open and close double quotes
# and move to just after the open quote
"\C-x\"": "\"\"\C-b"
# insert a backslash (testing backslash escapes
# in sequences and macros)
"\C-x\\": "\\"
# Quote the current or previous word
"\C-xq": "\eb\"\ef\""
# Add a binding to refresh the line, which is unbound
"\C-xr": redraw-current-line
# Edit variable on current line.
"\M-\C-v": "\C-a\C-k$\C-y\M-\C-e\C-a\C-y="
$endif

# use a visible bell if one is available
set bell-style visible

# don't strip characters to 7 bits when reading
set input-meta on

# allow iso-latin1 characters to be inserted rather
# than converted to prefix-meta sequences
set convert-meta off

# display characters with the eighth bit set directly
# rather than as meta-prefixed characters
set output-meta on

# if there are more than 150 possible completions for
# a word, ask the user if he wants to see all of them
set completion-query-items 150
```

```
# For FTP
$if Ftp
"\C-xg": "get \M-?"
"\C-xt": "put \M-?"
"\M-.": yank-last-arg
$endif
```

8.4 Bindable Readline Commands

This section describes Readline commands that may be bound to key sequences. You can list your key bindings by executing `bind -P` or, for a more terse format, suitable for an *inputrc* file, `bind -p`. (See Section 4.2 [Bash Builtins], page 49.) Command names without an accompanying key sequence are unbound by default.

In the following descriptions, *point* refers to the current cursor position, and *mark* refers to a cursor position saved by the `set-mark` command. The text between the point and mark is referred to as the *region*.

8.4.1 Commands For Moving

`beginning-of-line (C-a)`
> Move to the start of the current line.

`end-of-line (C-e)`
> Move to the end of the line.

`forward-char (C-f)`
> Move forward a character.

`backward-char (C-b)`
> Move back a character.

`forward-word (M-f)`
> Move forward to the end of the next word. Words are composed of letters and digits.

`backward-word (M-b)`
> Move back to the start of the current or previous word. Words are composed of letters and digits.

`shell-forward-word ()`
> Move forward to the end of the next word. Words are delimited by non-quoted shell metacharacters.

`shell-backward-word ()`
> Move back to the start of the current or previous word. Words are delimited by non-quoted shell metacharacters.

`clear-screen (C-l)`
> Clear the screen and redraw the current line, leaving the current line at the top of the screen.

`redraw-current-line ()`
> Refresh the current line. By default, this is unbound.

8.4.2 Commands For Manipulating The History

accept-line (Newline or Return)
> Accept the line regardless of where the cursor is. If this line is non-empty, add it to the history list according to the setting of the HISTCONTROL and HISTIGNORE variables. If this line is a modified history line, then restore the history line to its original state.

previous-history (C-p)
> Move 'back' through the history list, fetching the previous command.

next-history (C-n)
> Move 'forward' through the history list, fetching the next command.

beginning-of-history (M-<)
> Move to the first line in the history.

end-of-history (M->)
> Move to the end of the input history, i.e., the line currently being entered.

reverse-search-history (C-r)
> Search backward starting at the current line and moving 'up' through the history as necessary. This is an incremental search.

forward-search-history (C-s)
> Search forward starting at the current line and moving 'down' through the history as necessary. This is an incremental search.

non-incremental-reverse-search-history (M-p)
> Search backward starting at the current line and moving 'up' through the history as necessary using a non-incremental search for a string supplied by the user. The search string may match anywhere in a history line.

non-incremental-forward-search-history (M-n)
> Search forward starting at the current line and moving 'down' through the history as necessary using a non-incremental search for a string supplied by the user. The search string may match anywhere in a history line.

history-search-forward ()
> Search forward through the history for the string of characters between the start of the current line and the point. The search string must match at the beginning of a history line. This is a non-incremental search. By default, this command is unbound.

history-search-backward ()
> Search backward through the history for the string of characters between the start of the current line and the point. The search string must match at the beginning of a history line. This is a non-incremental search. By default, this command is unbound.

history-substr-search-forward ()
> Search forward through the history for the string of characters between the start of the current line and the point. The search string may match anywhere

in a history line. This is a non-incremental search. By default, this command
is unbound.

`history-substr-search-backward ()`

> Search backward through the history for the string of characters between the
> start of the current line and the point. The search string may match anywhere
> in a history line. This is a non-incremental search. By default, this command
> is unbound.

`yank-nth-arg (M-C-y)`

> Insert the first argument to the previous command (usually the second word
> on the previous line) at point. With an argument n, insert the nth word from
> the previous command (the words in the previous command begin with word
> 0). A negative argument inserts the nth word from the end of the previous
> command. Once the argument n is computed, the argument is extracted as if
> the '`!n`' history expansion had been specified.

`yank-last-arg (M-. or M-_)`

> Insert last argument to the previous command (the last word of the previous
> history entry). With a numeric argument, behave exactly like `yank-nth-arg`.
> Successive calls to `yank-last-arg` move back through the history list, inserting
> the last word (or the word specified by the argument to the first call) of each line
> in turn. Any numeric argument supplied to these successive calls determines
> the direction to move through the history. A negative argument switches the
> direction through the history (back or forward). The history expansion facilities
> are used to extract the last argument, as if the '`!$`' history expansion had been
> specified.

8.4.3 Commands For Changing Text

`end-of-file` (usually C-d)

> The character indicating end-of-file as set, for example, by `stty`. If this charac-
> ter is read when there are no characters on the line, and point is at the beginning
> of the line, Readline interprets it as the end of input and returns EOF.

`delete-char (C-d)`

> Delete the character at point. If this function is bound to the same character
> as the tty EOF character, as *C-d* commonly is, see above for the effects.

`backward-delete-char (Rubout)`

> Delete the character behind the cursor. A numeric argument means to kill the
> characters instead of deleting them.

`forward-backward-delete-char ()`

> Delete the character under the cursor, unless the cursor is at the end of the
> line, in which case the character behind the cursor is deleted. By default, this
> is not bound to a key.

`quoted-insert (C-q or C-v)`

> Add the next character typed to the line verbatim. This is how to insert key
> sequences like *C-q*, for example.

`self-insert (a, b, A, 1, !, ...)`
> Insert yourself.

`bracketed-paste-begin ()`
> This function is intended to be bound to the "bracketed paste" escape sequence sent by some terminals, and such a binding is assigned by default. It allows Readline to insert the pasted text as a single unit without treating each character as if it had been read from the keyboard. The characters are inserted as if each one was bound to **self-insert**) instead of executing any editing commands.

`transpose-chars (C-t)`
> Drag the character before the cursor forward over the character at the cursor, moving the cursor forward as well. If the insertion point is at the end of the line, then this transposes the last two characters of the line. Negative arguments have no effect.

`transpose-words (M-t)`
> Drag the word before point past the word after point, moving point past that word as well. If the insertion point is at the end of the line, this transposes the last two words on the line.

`upcase-word (M-u)`
> Uppercase the current (or following) word. With a negative argument, uppercase the previous word, but do not move the cursor.

`downcase-word (M-l)`
> Lowercase the current (or following) word. With a negative argument, lowercase the previous word, but do not move the cursor.

`capitalize-word (M-c)`
> Capitalize the current (or following) word. With a negative argument, capitalize the previous word, but do not move the cursor.

`overwrite-mode ()`
> Toggle overwrite mode. With an explicit positive numeric argument, switches to overwrite mode. With an explicit non-positive numeric argument, switches to insert mode. This command affects only **emacs** mode; **vi** mode does overwrite differently. Each call to **readline()** starts in insert mode.
>
> In overwrite mode, characters bound to **self-insert** replace the text at point rather than pushing the text to the right. Characters bound to **backward-delete-char** replace the character before point with a space.
>
> By default, this command is unbound.

8.4.4 Killing And Yanking

`kill-line (C-k)`
> Kill the text from point to the end of the line.

`backward-kill-line (C-x Rubout)`
> Kill backward from the cursor to the beginning of the current line.

`unix-line-discard (C-u)`
> Kill backward from the cursor to the beginning of the current line.

`kill-whole-line ()`
> Kill all characters on the current line, no matter where point is. By default, this is unbound.

`kill-word (M-d)`
> Kill from point to the end of the current word, or if between words, to the end of the next word. Word boundaries are the same as `forward-word`.

`backward-kill-word (M-DEL)`
> Kill the word behind point. Word boundaries are the same as `backward-word`.

`shell-kill-word ()`
> Kill from point to the end of the current word, or if between words, to the end of the next word. Word boundaries are the same as `shell-forward-word`.

`shell-backward-kill-word ()`
> Kill the word behind point. Word boundaries are the same as `shell-backward-word`.

`unix-word-rubout (C-w)`
> Kill the word behind point, using white space as a word boundary. The killed text is saved on the kill-ring.

`unix-filename-rubout ()`
> Kill the word behind point, using white space and the slash character as the word boundaries. The killed text is saved on the kill-ring.

`delete-horizontal-space ()`
> Delete all spaces and tabs around point. By default, this is unbound.

`kill-region ()`
> Kill the text in the current region. By default, this command is unbound.

`copy-region-as-kill ()`
> Copy the text in the region to the kill buffer, so it can be yanked right away. By default, this command is unbound.

`copy-backward-word ()`
> Copy the word before point to the kill buffer. The word boundaries are the same as `backward-word`. By default, this command is unbound.

`copy-forward-word ()`
> Copy the word following point to the kill buffer. The word boundaries are the same as `forward-word`. By default, this command is unbound.

`yank (C-y)`
> Yank the top of the kill ring into the buffer at point.

`yank-pop (M-y)`
> Rotate the kill-ring, and yank the new top. You can only do this if the prior command is `yank` or `yank-pop`.

8.4.5 Specifying Numeric Arguments

digit-argument (M-0, M-1, ... M--)

>Add this digit to the argument already accumulating, or start a new argument. M-- starts a negative argument.

universal-argument ()

>This is another way to specify an argument. If this command is followed by one or more digits, optionally with a leading minus sign, those digits define the argument. If the command is followed by digits, executing universal-argument again ends the numeric argument, but is otherwise ignored. As a special case, if this command is immediately followed by a character that is neither a digit nor minus sign, the argument count for the next command is multiplied by four. The argument count is initially one, so executing this function the first time makes the argument count four, a second time makes the argument count sixteen, and so on. By default, this is not bound to a key.

8.4.6 Letting Readline Type For You

complete (TAB)

>Attempt to perform completion on the text before point. The actual completion performed is application-specific. Bash attempts completion treating the text as a variable (if the text begins with '$'), username (if the text begins with '~'), hostname (if the text begins with '@'), or command (including aliases and functions) in turn. If none of these produces a match, filename completion is attempted.

possible-completions (M-?)

>List the possible completions of the text before point. When displaying completions, Readline sets the number of columns used for display to the value of completion-display-width, the value of the environment variable COLUMNS, or the screen width, in that order.

insert-completions (M-*)

>Insert all completions of the text before point that would have been generated by possible-completions.

menu-complete ()

>Similar to complete, but replaces the word to be completed with a single match from the list of possible completions. Repeated execution of menu-complete steps through the list of possible completions, inserting each match in turn. At the end of the list of completions, the bell is rung (subject to the setting of bell-style) and the original text is restored. An argument of n moves n positions forward in the list of matches; a negative argument may be used to move backward through the list. This command is intended to be bound to TAB, but is unbound by default.

menu-complete-backward ()

>Identical to menu-complete, but moves backward through the list of possible completions, as if menu-complete had been given a negative argument.

`delete-char-or-list ()`

> Deletes the character under the cursor if not at the beginning or end of the line (like `delete-char`). If at the end of the line, behaves identically to `possible-completions`. This command is unbound by default.

`complete-filename (M-/)`

> Attempt filename completion on the text before point.

`possible-filename-completions (C-x /)`

> List the possible completions of the text before point, treating it as a filename.

`complete-username (M-~)`

> Attempt completion on the text before point, treating it as a username.

`possible-username-completions (C-x ~)`

> List the possible completions of the text before point, treating it as a username.

`complete-variable (M-$)`

> Attempt completion on the text before point, treating it as a shell variable.

`possible-variable-completions (C-x $)`

> List the possible completions of the text before point, treating it as a shell variable.

`complete-hostname (M-@)`

> Attempt completion on the text before point, treating it as a hostname.

`possible-hostname-completions (C-x @)`

> List the possible completions of the text before point, treating it as a hostname.

`complete-command (M-!)`

> Attempt completion on the text before point, treating it as a command name. Command completion attempts to match the text against aliases, reserved words, shell functions, shell builtins, and finally executable filenames, in that order.

`possible-command-completions (C-x !)`

> List the possible completions of the text before point, treating it as a command name.

`dynamic-complete-history (M-TAB)`

> Attempt completion on the text before point, comparing the text against lines from the history list for possible completion matches.

`dabbrev-expand ()`

> Attempt menu completion on the text before point, comparing the text against lines from the history list for possible completion matches.

`complete-into-braces (M-{)`

> Perform filename completion and insert the list of possible completions enclosed within braces so the list is available to the shell (see Section 3.5.1 [Brace Expansion], page 21).

8.4.7 Keyboard Macros

`start-kbd-macro (C-x ()`
> Begin saving the characters typed into the current keyboard macro.

`end-kbd-macro (C-x ))`
> Stop saving the characters typed into the current keyboard macro and save the definition.

`call-last-kbd-macro (C-x e)`
> Re-execute the last keyboard macro defined, by making the characters in the macro appear as if typed at the keyboard.

`print-last-kbd-macro ()`
> Print the last keboard macro defined in a format suitable for the *inputrc* file.

8.4.8 Some Miscellaneous Commands

`re-read-init-file (C-x C-r)`
> Read in the contents of the *inputrc* file, and incorporate any bindings or variable assignments found there.

`abort (C-g)`
> Abort the current editing command and ring the terminal's bell (subject to the setting of `bell-style`).

`do-uppercase-version (M-a, M-b, M-x, ...)`
> If the metafied character *x* is lowercase, run the command that is bound to the corresponding uppercase character.

`prefix-meta (ESC)`
> Metafy the next character typed. This is for keyboards without a meta key. Typing 'ESC f' is equivalent to typing *M-f*.

`undo (C-_ or C-x C-u)`
> Incremental undo, separately remembered for each line.

`revert-line (M-r)`
> Undo all changes made to this line. This is like executing the **undo** command enough times to get back to the beginning.

`tilde-expand (M-&)`
> Perform tilde expansion on the current word.

`set-mark (C-@)`
> Set the mark to the point. If a numeric argument is supplied, the mark is set to that position.

`exchange-point-and-mark (C-x C-x)`
> Swap the point with the mark. The current cursor position is set to the saved position, and the old cursor position is saved as the mark.

`character-search (C-])`
> A character is read and point is moved to the next occurrence of that character. A negative count searches for previous occurrences.

`character-search-backward (M-C-])`

> A character is read and point is moved to the previous occurrence of that character. A negative count searches for subsequent occurrences.

`skip-csi-sequence ()`

> Read enough characters to consume a multi-key sequence such as those defined for keys like Home and End. Such sequences begin with a Control Sequence Indicator (CSI), usually ESC-[. If this sequence is bound to "\e[", keys producing such sequences will have no effect unless explicitly bound to a readline command, instead of inserting stray characters into the editing buffer. This is unbound by default, but usually bound to ESC-[.

`insert-comment (M-#)`

> Without a numeric argument, the value of the **comment-begin** variable is inserted at the beginning of the current line. If a numeric argument is supplied, this command acts as a toggle: if the characters at the beginning of the line do not match the value of **comment-begin**, the value is inserted, otherwise the characters in **comment-begin** are deleted from the beginning of the line. In either case, the line is accepted as if a newline had been typed. The default value of **comment-begin** causes this command to make the current line a shell comment. If a numeric argument causes the comment character to be removed, the line will be executed by the shell.

`dump-functions ()`

> Print all of the functions and their key bindings to the Readline output stream. If a numeric argument is supplied, the output is formatted in such a way that it can be made part of an *inputrc* file. This command is unbound by default.

`dump-variables ()`

> Print all of the settable variables and their values to the Readline output stream. If a numeric argument is supplied, the output is formatted in such a way that it can be made part of an *inputrc* file. This command is unbound by default.

`dump-macros ()`

> Print all of the Readline key sequences bound to macros and the strings they output. If a numeric argument is supplied, the output is formatted in such a way that it can be made part of an *inputrc* file. This command is unbound by default.

`glob-complete-word (M-g)`

> The word before point is treated as a pattern for pathname expansion, with an asterisk implicitly appended. This pattern is used to generate a list of matching file names for possible completions.

`glob-expand-word (C-x *)`

> The word before point is treated as a pattern for pathname expansion, and the list of matching file names is inserted, replacing the word. If a numeric argument is supplied, a '*' is appended before pathname expansion.

`glob-list-expansions (C-x g)`

> The list of expansions that would have been generated by `glob-expand-word` is displayed, and the line is redrawn. If a numeric argument is supplied, a '*' is appended before pathname expansion.

`display-shell-version (C-x C-v)`

> Display version information about the current instance of Bash.

`shell-expand-line (M-C-e)`

> Expand the line as the shell does. This performs alias and history expansion as well as all of the shell word expansions (see Section 3.5 [Shell Expansions], page 21).

`history-expand-line (M-^)`

> Perform history expansion on the current line.

`magic-space ()`

> Perform history expansion on the current line and insert a space (see Section 9.3 [History Interaction], page 139).

`alias-expand-line ()`

> Perform alias expansion on the current line (see Section 6.6 [Aliases], page 90).

`history-and-alias-expand-line ()`

> Perform history and alias expansion on the current line.

`insert-last-argument (M-. or M-_)`

> A synonym for `yank-last-arg`.

`operate-and-get-next (C-o)`

> Accept the current line for execution and fetch the next line relative to the current line from the history for editing. Any argument is ignored.

`edit-and-execute-command (C-xC-e)`

> Invoke an editor on the current command line, and execute the result as shell commands. Bash attempts to invoke `$VISUAL`, `$EDITOR`, and `emacs` as the editor, in that order.

8.5 Readline vi Mode

While the Readline library does not have a full set of `vi` editing functions, it does contain enough to allow simple editing of the line. The Readline `vi` mode behaves as specified in the POSIX standard.

In order to switch interactively between `emacs` and `vi` editing modes, use the 'set -o emacs' and 'set -o vi' commands (see Section 4.3.1 [The Set Builtin], page 60). The Readline default is `emacs` mode.

When you enter a line in `vi` mode, you are already placed in 'insertion' mode, as if you had typed an 'i'. Pressing ESC switches you into 'command' mode, where you can edit the text of the line with the standard `vi` movement keys, move to previous history lines with 'k' and subsequent lines with 'j', and so forth.

8.6 Programmable Completion

When word completion is attempted for an argument to a command for which a completion specification (a *compspec*) has been defined using the **complete** builtin (see Section 8.7 [Programmable Completion Builtins], page 131), the programmable completion facilities are invoked.

First, the command name is identified. If a compspec has been defined for that command, the compspec is used to generate the list of possible completions for the word. If the command word is the empty string (completion attempted at the beginning of an empty line), any compspec defined with the **-E** option to **complete** is used. If the command word is a full pathname, a compspec for the full pathname is searched for first. If no compspec is found for the full pathname, an attempt is made to find a compspec for the portion following the final slash. If those searches do not result in a compspec, any compspec defined with the **-D** option to **complete** is used as the default.

Once a compspec has been found, it is used to generate the list of matching words. If a compspec is not found, the default Bash completion described above (see Section 8.4.6 [Commands For Completion], page 124) is performed.

First, the actions specified by the compspec are used. Only matches which are prefixed by the word being completed are returned. When the **-f** or **-d** option is used for filename or directory name completion, the shell variable **FIGNORE** is used to filter the matches. See Section 5.2 [Bash Variables], page 71, for a description of **FIGNORE**.

Any completions specified by a filename expansion pattern to the **-G** option are generated next. The words generated by the pattern need not match the word being completed. The **GLOBIGNORE** shell variable is not used to filter the matches, but the **FIGNORE** shell variable is used.

Next, the string specified as the argument to the **-W** option is considered. The string is first split using the characters in the **IFS** special variable as delimiters. Shell quoting is honored. Each word is then expanded using brace expansion, tilde expansion, parameter and variable expansion, command substitution, and arithmetic expansion, as described above (see Section 3.5 [Shell Expansions], page 21). The results are split using the rules described above (see Section 3.5.7 [Word Splitting], page 30). The results of the expansion are prefix-matched against the word being completed, and the matching words become the possible completions.

After these matches have been generated, any shell function or command specified with the **-F** and **-C** options is invoked. When the command or function is invoked, the **COMP_LINE**, **COMP_POINT**, **COMP_KEY**, and **COMP_TYPE** variables are assigned values as described above (see Section 5.2 [Bash Variables], page 71). If a shell function is being invoked, the **COMP_WORDS** and **COMP_CWORD** variables are also set. When the function or command is invoked, the first argument ($1) is the name of the command whose arguments are being completed, the second argument ($2) is the word being completed, and the third argument ($3) is the word preceding the word being completed on the current command line. No filtering of the generated completions against the word being completed is performed; the function or command has complete freedom in generating the matches.

Any function specified with **-F** is invoked first. The function may use any of the shell facilities, including the **compgen** and **compopt** builtins described below (see Section 8.7

[Programmable Completion Builtins], page 131), to generate the matches. It must put the possible completions in the COMPREPLY array variable, one per array element.

Next, any command specified with the -C option is invoked in an environment equivalent to command substitution. It should print a list of completions, one per line, to the standard output. Backslash may be used to escape a newline, if necessary.

After all of the possible completions are generated, any filter specified with the -X option is applied to the list. The filter is a pattern as used for pathname expansion; a '&' in the pattern is replaced with the text of the word being completed. A literal '&' may be escaped with a backslash; the backslash is removed before attempting a match. Any completion that matches the pattern will be removed from the list. A leading '!' negates the pattern; in this case any completion not matching the pattern will be removed. If the **nocasematch** shell option (see the description of **shopt** in Section 4.3.2 [The Shopt Builtin], page 64) is enabled, the match is performed without regard to the case of alphabetic characters.

Finally, any prefix and suffix specified with the -P and -S options are added to each member of the completion list, and the result is returned to the Readline completion code as the list of possible completions.

If the previously-applied actions do not generate any matches, and the -o **dirnames** option was supplied to **complete** when the compspec was defined, directory name completion is attempted.

If the -o **plusdirs** option was supplied to **complete** when the compspec was defined, directory name completion is attempted and any matches are added to the results of the other actions.

By default, if a compspec is found, whatever it generates is returned to the completion code as the full set of possible completions. The default Bash completions are not attempted, and the Readline default of filename completion is disabled. If the -o **bashdefault** option was supplied to **complete** when the compspec was defined, the default Bash completions are attempted if the compspec generates no matches. If the -o **default** option was supplied to **complete** when the compspec was defined, Readline's default completion will be performed if the compspec (and, if attempted, the default Bash completions) generate no matches.

When a compspec indicates that directory name completion is desired, the programmable completion functions force Readline to append a slash to completed names which are symbolic links to directories, subject to the value of the *mark-directories* Readline variable, regardless of the setting of the *mark-symlinked-directories* Readline variable.

There is some support for dynamically modifying completions. This is most useful when used in combination with a default completion specified with -D. It's possible for shell functions executed as completion handlers to indicate that completion should be retried by returning an exit status of 124. If a shell function returns 124, and changes the compspec associated with the command on which completion is being attempted (supplied as the first argument when the function is executed), programmable completion restarts from the beginning, with an attempt to find a new compspec for that command. This allows a set of completions to be built dynamically as completion is attempted, rather than being loaded all at once.

For instance, assuming that there is a library of compspecs, each kept in a file corresponding to the name of the command, the following default completion function would load completions dynamically:

```
_completion_loader()
{
    . "/etc/bash_completion.d/$1.sh" >/dev/null 2>&1 && return 124
}
complete -D -F _completion_loader -o bashdefault -o default
```

8.7 Programmable Completion Builtins

Three builtin commands are available to manipulate the programmable completion facilities:
one to specify how the arguments to a particular command are to be completed, and two
to modify the completion as it is happening.

compgen

> `compgen [option] [word]`
>
> Generate possible completion matches for *word* according to the *option*s, which
> may be any option accepted by the `complete` builtin with the exception of `-p`
> and `-r`, and write the matches to the standard output. When using the `-F`
> or `-C` options, the various shell variables set by the programmable completion
> facilities, while available, will not have useful values.
>
> The matches will be generated in the same way as if the programmable com-
> pletion code had generated them directly from a completion specification with
> the same flags. If *word* is specified, only those completions matching *word* will
> be displayed.
>
> The return value is true unless an invalid option is supplied, or no matches were
> generated.

complete

> `complete [-abcdefgjksuv] [-o comp-option] [-DE] [-A action] [-`
> `G globpat] [-W wordlist]`
> `[-F function] [-C command] [-X filterpat]`
> `[-P prefix] [-S suffix] name [name ...]`
> `complete -pr [-DE] [name ...]`
>
> Specify how arguments to each *name* should be completed. If the `-p` option
> is supplied, or if no options are supplied, existing completion specifications are
> printed in a way that allows them to be reused as input. The `-r` option removes
> a completion specification for each *name*, or, if no *name*s are supplied, all com-
> pletion specifications. The `-D` option indicates that the remaining options and
> actions should apply to the "default" command completion; that is, completion
> attempted on a command for which no completion has previously been defined.
> The `-E` option indicates that the remaining options and actions should apply to
> "empty" command completion; that is, completion attempted on a blank line.
>
> The process of applying these completion specifications when word completion
> is attempted is described above (see Section 8.6 [Programmable Completion],
> page 129). The `-D` option takes precedence over `-E`.
>
> Other options, if specified, have the following meanings. The arguments to the
> `-G`, `-W`, and `-X` options (and, if necessary, the `-P` and `-S` options) should be
> quoted to protect them from expansion before the `complete` builtin is invoked.

-o *comp-option*

The *comp-option* controls several aspects of the compspec's behavior beyond the simple generation of completions. *comp-option* may be one of:

bashdefault
> Perform the rest of the default Bash completions if the compspec generates no matches.

default Use Readline's default filename completion if the compspec generates no matches.

dirnames Perform directory name completion if the compspec generates no matches.

filenames
> Tell Readline that the compspec generates filenames, so it can perform any filename-specific processing (like adding a slash to directory names quoting special characters, or suppressing trailing spaces). This option is intended to be used with shell functions specified with **-F**.

noquote Tell Readline not to quote the completed words if they are filenames (quoting filenames is the default).

nosort Tell Readline not to sort the list of possible completions alphabetically.

nospace Tell Readline not to append a space (the default) to words completed at the end of the line.

plusdirs After any matches defined by the compspec are generated, directory name completion is attempted and any matches are added to the results of the other actions.

-A *action* The *action* may be one of the following to generate a list of possible completions:

alias Alias names. May also be specified as **-a**.

arrayvar Array variable names.

binding Readline key binding names (see Section 8.4 [Bindable Readline Commands], page 119).

builtin Names of shell builtin commands. May also be specified as **-b**.

command Command names. May also be specified as **-c**.

directory
> Directory names. May also be specified as **-d**.

disabled Names of disabled shell builtins.

enabled Names of enabled shell builtins.

export   Names of exported shell variables. May also be specified as -e.

file   File names. May also be specified as -f.

function   Names of shell functions.

group   Group names. May also be specified as -g.

helptopic
              Help topics as accepted by the **help** builtin (see Section 4.2 [Bash Builtins], page 49).

hostname   Hostnames, as taken from the file specified by the **HOSTFILE** shell variable (see Section 5.2 [Bash Variables], page 71).

job   Job names, if job control is active. May also be specified as -j.

keyword   Shell reserved words. May also be specified as -k.

running   Names of running jobs, if job control is active.

service   Service names. May also be specified as -s.

setopt   Valid arguments for the -o option to the **set** builtin (see Section 4.3.1 [The Set Builtin], page 60).

shopt   Shell option names as accepted by the **shopt** builtin (see Section 4.2 [Bash Builtins], page 49).

signal   Signal names.

stopped   Names of stopped jobs, if job control is active.

user   User names. May also be specified as -u.

variable   Names of all shell variables. May also be specified as -v.

-C *command*

> *command* is executed in a subshell environment, and its output is used as the possible completions.

-F *function*

> The shell function *function* is executed in the current shell environment. When it is executed, $1 is the name of the command whose arguments are being completed, $2 is the word being completed, and $3 is the word preceding the word being completed, as described above (see Section 8.6 [Programmable Completion], page 129). When it finishes, the possible completions are retrieved from the value of the **COMPREPLY** array variable.

-G *globpat*

> The filename expansion pattern *globpat* is expanded to generate the possible completions.

-P *prefix*   *prefix* is added at the beginning of each possible completion after all other options have been applied.

-S *suffix*   *suffix* is appended to each possible completion after all other options have been applied.

-W *wordlist*

The *wordlist* is split using the characters in the IFS special variable as delimiters, and each resultant word is expanded. The possible completions are the members of the resultant list which match the word being completed.

-X *filterpat*

filterpat is a pattern as used for filename expansion. It is applied to the list of possible completions generated by the preceding options and arguments, and each completion matching *filterpat* is removed from the list. A leading '!' in *filterpat* negates the pattern; in this case, any completion not matching *filterpat* is removed.

The return value is true unless an invalid option is supplied, an option other than -p or -r is supplied without a *name* argument, an attempt is made to remove a completion specification for a *name* for which no specification exists, or an error occurs adding a completion specification.

compopt

compopt [-o *option*] [-DE] [+o *option*] [*name*]

Modify completion options for each *name* according to the *option*s, or for the currently-executing completion if no *name*s are supplied. If no *option*s are given, display the completion options for each *name* or the current completion. The possible values of *option* are those valid for the complete builtin described above. The -D option indicates that the remaining options should apply to the "default" command completion; that is, completion attempted on a command for which no completion has previously been defined. The -E option indicates that the remaining options should apply to "empty" command completion; that is, completion attempted on a blank line.

The -D option takes precedence over -E.

The return value is true unless an invalid option is supplied, an attempt is made to modify the options for a *name* for which no completion specification exists, or an output error occurs.

8.8 A Programmable Completion Example

The most common way to obtain additional completion functionality beyond the default actions complete and compgen provide is to use a shell function and bind it to a particular command using complete -F.

The following function provides completions for the cd builtin. It is a reasonably good example of what shell functions must do when used for completion. This function uses the word passsed as $2 to determine the directory name to complete. You can also use the COMP_WORDS array variable; the current word is indexed by the COMP_CWORD variable.

The function relies on the **complete** and **compgen** builtins to do much of the work, adding only the things that the Bash **cd** does beyond accepting basic directory names: tilde expansion (see Section 3.5.2 [Tilde Expansion], page 22), searching directories in *$CDPATH*, which is described above (see Section 4.1 [Bourne Shell Builtins], page 42), and basic support for the **cdable_vars** shell option (see Section 4.3.2 [The Shopt Builtin], page 64). **_comp_ cd** modifies the value of *IFS* so that it contains only a newline to accommodate file names containing spaces and tabs – **compgen** prints the possible completions it generates one per line.

Possible completions go into the *COMPREPLY* array variable, one completion per array element. The programmable completion system retrieves the completions from there when the function returns.

```
# A completion function for the cd builtin
# based on the cd completion function from the bash_completion package
_comp_cd()
{
    local IFS=$' \t\n'     # normalize IFS
    local cur _skipdot _cdpath
    local i j k

    # Tilde expansion, with side effect of expanding tilde to full pathname
    case "$2" in
    \~*)    eval cur="$2" ;;
    *)      cur=$2 ;;
    esac

    # no cdpath or absolute pathname -- straight directory completion
    if [[ -z "${CDPATH:-}" ]] || [[ "$cur" == @(./*|../*|/*) ]]; then
        # compgen prints paths one per line; could also use while loop
        IFS=$'\n'
        COMPREPLY=( $(compgen -d -- "$cur") )
        IFS=$' \t\n'
    # CDPATH+directories in the current directory if not in CDPATH
    else
        IFS=$'\n'
        _skipdot=false
        # preprocess CDPATH to convert null directory names to .
        _cdpath=${CDPATH/#:/.:}
        _cdpath=${_cdpath//::/:.:}
        _cdpath=${_cdpath/%:/:.}
        for i in ${_cdpath//:/$'\n'}; do
            if [[ $i -ef . ]]; then _skipdot=true; fi
            k="${#COMPREPLY[@]}"
            for j in $( compgen -d -- "$i/$cur" ); do
                COMPREPLY[k++]=${j#$i/}        # cut off directory
            done
        done
```

```
        $_skipdot || COMPREPLY+=( $(compgen -d -- "$cur") )
        IFS=$' \t\n'
fi

# variable names if appropriate shell option set and no completions
if shopt -q cdable_vars && [[ ${#COMPREPLY[@]} -eq 0 ]]; then
    COMPREPLY=( $(compgen -v -- "$cur") )
fi

return 0
}
```

We install the completion function using the -F option to `complete`:

```
# Tell readline to quote appropriate and append slashes to directories;
# use the bash default completion for other arguments
complete -o filenames -o nospace -o bashdefault -F _comp_cd cd
```

Since we'd like Bash and Readline to take care of some of the other details for us, we use several other options to tell Bash and Readline what to do. The -o `filenames` option tells Readline that the possible completions should be treated as filenames, and quoted appropriately. That option will also cause Readline to append a slash to filenames it can determine are directories (which is why we might want to extend `_comp_cd` to append a slash if we're using directories found via *CDPATH*: Readline can't tell those completions are directories). The -o `nospace` option tells Readline to not append a space character to the directory name, in case we want to append to it. The -o `bashdefault` option brings in the rest of the "Bash default" completions – possible completion that Bash adds to the default Readline set. These include things like command name completion, variable completion for words beginning with '{', completions containing pathname expansion patterns (see Section 3.5.8 [Filename Expansion], page 30), and so on.

Once installed using `complete`, `_comp_cd` will be called every time we attempt word completion for a `cd` command.

Many more examples – an extensive collection of completions for most of the common GNU, Unix, and Linux commands – are available as part of the bash_completion project. This is installed by default on many GNU/Linux distributions. Originally written by Ian Macdonald, the project now lives at `http://bash-completion.alioth.debian.org/`. There are ports for other systems such as Solaris and Mac OS X.

An older version of the bash_completion package is distributed with bash in the `examples/complete` subdirectory.

9 Using History Interactively

This chapter describes how to use the GNU History Library interactively, from a user's standpoint. It should be considered a user's guide. For information on using the GNU History Library in other programs, see the GNU Readline Library Manual.

9.1 Bash History Facilities

When the -o history option to the set builtin is enabled (see Section 4.3.1 [The Set Builtin], page 60), the shell provides access to the *command history*, the list of commands previously typed. The value of the HISTSIZE shell variable is used as the number of commands to save in a history list. The text of the last $HISTSIZE commands (default 500) is saved. The shell stores each command in the history list prior to parameter and variable expansion but after history expansion is performed, subject to the values of the shell variables HISTIGNORE and HISTCONTROL.

When the shell starts up, the history is initialized from the file named by the HISTFILE variable (default ~/.bash_history). The file named by the value of HISTFILE is truncated, if necessary, to contain no more than the number of lines specified by the value of the HISTFILESIZE variable. When a shell with history enabled exits, the last $HISTSIZE lines are copied from the history list to the file named by $HISTFILE. If the histappend shell option is set (see Section 4.2 [Bash Builtins], page 49), the lines are appended to the history file, otherwise the history file is overwritten. If HISTFILE is unset, or if the history file is unwritable, the history is not saved. After saving the history, the history file is truncated to contain no more than $HISTFILESIZE lines. If HISTFILESIZE is unset, or set to null, a non-numeric value, or a numeric value less than zero, the history file is not truncated.

If the HISTTIMEFORMAT is set, the time stamp information associated with each history entry is written to the history file, marked with the history comment character. When the history file is read, lines beginning with the history comment character followed immediately by a digit are interpreted as timestamps for the following history entry.

The builtin command fc may be used to list or edit and re-execute a portion of the history list. The history builtin may be used to display or modify the history list and manipulate the history file. When using command-line editing, search commands are available in each editing mode that provide access to the history list (see Section 8.4.2 [Commands For History], page 120).

The shell allows control over which commands are saved on the history list. The HISTCONTROL and HISTIGNORE variables may be set to cause the shell to save only a subset of the commands entered. The cmdhist shell option, if enabled, causes the shell to attempt to save each line of a multi-line command in the same history entry, adding semicolons where necessary to preserve syntactic correctness. The lithist shell option causes the shell to save the command with embedded newlines instead of semicolons. The shopt builtin is used to set these options. See Section 4.2 [Bash Builtins], page 49, for a description of shopt.

9.2 Bash History Builtins

Bash provides two builtin commands which manipulate the history list and history file.

fc

        fc [-e ename] [-lnr] [first] [last]

```
fc -s [pat=rep] [command]
```

The first form selects a range of commands from *first* to *last* from the history list and displays or edits and re-executes them. Both *first* and *last* may be specified as a string (to locate the most recent command beginning with that string) or as a number (an index into the history list, where a negative number is used as an offset from the current command number). If *last* is not specified it is set to *first*. If *first* is not specified it is set to the previous command for editing and −16 for listing. If the -l flag is given, the commands are listed on standard output. The -n flag suppresses the command numbers when listing. The -r flag reverses the order of the listing. Otherwise, the editor given by *ename* is invoked on a file containing those commands. If *ename* is not given, the value of the following variable expansion is used: ${FCEDIT:-${EDITOR:-vi}}. This says to use the value of the FCEDIT variable if set, or the value of the EDITOR variable if that is set, or vi if neither is set. When editing is complete, the edited commands are echoed and executed.

In the second form, *command* is re-executed after each instance of *pat* in the selected command is replaced by *rep*. *command* is intepreted the same as *first* above.

A useful alias to use with the fc command is r='fc -s', so that typing 'r cc' runs the last command beginning with cc and typing 'r' re-executes the last command (see Section 6.6 [Aliases], page 90).

history

```
history [n]
history -c
history -d offset
history [-anrw] [filename]
history -ps arg
```

With no options, display the history list with line numbers. Lines prefixed with a '*' have been modified. An argument of *n* lists only the last *n* lines. If the shell variable HISTTIMEFORMAT is set and not null, it is used as a format string for *strftime* to display the time stamp associated with each displayed history entry. No intervening blank is printed between the formatted time stamp and the history line.

Options, if supplied, have the following meanings:

-c   Clear the history list. This may be combined with the other options to replace the history list completely.

-d offset   Delete the history entry at position *offset*. *offset* should be specified as it appears when the history is displayed.

-a   Append the new history lines to the history file. These are history lines entered since the beginning of the current Bash session, but not already appended to the history file.

-n   Append the history lines not already read from the history file to the current history list. These are lines appended to the history file since the beginning of the current Bash session.

-r   Read the history file and append its contents to the history list.

-w   Write out the current history list to the history file.

-p   Perform history substitution on the *args* and display the result on the standard output, without storing the results in the history list.

-s   The *args* are added to the end of the history list as a single entry.

When any of the -w, -r, -a, or -n options is used, if *filename* is given, then it is used as the history file. If not, then the value of the **HISTFILE** variable is used.

9.3 History Expansion

The History library provides a history expansion feature that is similar to the history expansion provided by **csh**. This section describes the syntax used to manipulate the history information.

History expansions introduce words from the history list into the input stream, making it easy to repeat commands, insert the arguments to a previous command into the current input line, or fix errors in previous commands quickly.

History expansion is performed immediately after a complete line is read, before the shell breaks it into words.

History expansion takes place in two parts. The first is to determine which line from the history list should be used during substitution. The second is to select portions of that line for inclusion into the current one. The line selected from the history is called the *event*, and the portions of that line that are acted upon are called *words*. Various *modifiers* are available to manipulate the selected words. The line is broken into words in the same fashion that Bash does, so that several words surrounded by quotes are considered one word. History expansions are introduced by the appearance of the history expansion character, which is '!' by default. Only '\' and ' ' ' may be used to escape the history expansion character, but the history expansion character is also treated as quoted if it immediately precedes the closing double quote in a double-quoted string.

Several shell options settable with the **shopt** builtin (see Section 4.2 [Bash Builtins], page 49) may be used to tailor the behavior of history expansion. If the **histverify** shell option is enabled, and Readline is being used, history substitutions are not immediately passed to the shell parser. Instead, the expanded line is reloaded into the Readline editing buffer for further modification. If Readline is being used, and the **histreedit** shell option is enabled, a failed history expansion will be reloaded into the Readline editing buffer for correction. The -p option to the **history** builtin command may be used to see what a history expansion will do before using it. The -s option to the **history** builtin may be used to add commands to the end of the history list without actually executing them, so that they are available for subsequent recall. This is most useful in conjunction with Readline.

The shell allows control of the various characters used by the history expansion mechanism with the **histchars** variable, as explained above (see Section 5.2 [Bash Variables], page 71). The shell uses the history comment character to mark history timestamps when writing the history file.

9.3.1 Event Designators

An event designator is a reference to a command line entry in the history list. Unless the reference is absolute, events are relative to the current position in the history list.

!   Start a history substitution, except when followed by a space, tab, the end of the line, '=' or '(' (when the **extglob** shell option is enabled using the **shopt** builtin).

!*n*   Refer to command line *n*.

!-*n*   Refer to the command *n* lines back.

!!   Refer to the previous command. This is a synonym for '!-1'.

!*string*   Refer to the most recent command preceding the current position in the history list starting with *string*.

!?*string*[?]

Refer to the most recent command preceding the current position in the history list containing *string*. The trailing '?' may be omitted if the *string* is followed immediately by a newline.

^*string1*^*string2*^

Quick Substitution. Repeat the last command, replacing *string1* with *string2*. Equivalent to !!:s/*string1*/*string2*/.

!#   The entire command line typed so far.

9.3.2 Word Designators

Word designators are used to select desired words from the event. A ':' separates the event specification from the word designator. It may be omitted if the word designator begins with a '^', '$', '*', '-', or '%'. Words are numbered from the beginning of the line, with the first word being denoted by 0 (zero). Words are inserted into the current line separated by single spaces.

For example,

!!   designates the preceding command. When you type this, the preceding command is repeated in toto.

!!:$ designates the last argument of the preceding command. This may be shortened to !$.

!fi:2   designates the second argument of the most recent command starting with the letters **fi**.

Here are the word designators:

0 (**zero**)   The 0th word. For many applications, this is the command word.

n   The *n*th word.

^   The first argument; that is, word 1.

$ The last argument.

%   The word matched by the most recent '?*string*?' search.

x-y   A range of words; '-*y*' abbreviates '0-*y*'.

*   All of the words, except the 0th. This is a synonym for '1-$'. It is not an error to use '*' if there is just one word in the event; the empty string is returned in that case.

*x**   Abbreviates '*x*-$'

x-   Abbreviates '*x*-$' like '*x**', but omits the last word.

    If a word designator is supplied without an event specification, the previous command is used as the event.

9.3.3 Modifiers

After the optional word designator, you can add a sequence of one or more of the following modifiers, each preceded by a ':'.

h   Remove a trailing pathname component, leaving only the head.

t   Remove all leading pathname components, leaving the tail.

r   Remove a trailing suffix of the form '.*suffix*', leaving the basename.

e   Remove all but the trailing suffix.

p   Print the new command but do not execute it.

q   Quote the substituted words, escaping further substitutions.

x   Quote the substituted words as with 'q', but break into words at spaces, tabs, and newlines.

s/old/new/
          Substitute *new* for the first occurrence of *old* in the event line. Any delimiter may be used in place of '/'. The delimiter may be quoted in *old* and *new* with a single backslash. If '&' appears in *new*, it is replaced by *old*. A single backslash will quote the '&'. The final delimiter is optional if it is the last character on the input line.

&   Repeat the previous substitution.

g
a   Cause changes to be applied over the entire event line. Used in conjunction with 's', as in gs/*old*/*new*/, or with '&'.

G   Apply the following 's' modifier once to each word in the event.

10 Installing Bash

This chapter provides basic instructions for installing Bash on the various supported platforms. The distribution supports the GNU operating systems, nearly every version of Unix, and several non-Unix systems such as BeOS and Interix. Other independent ports exist for MS-DOS, OS/2, and Windows platforms.

10.1 Basic Installation

These are installation instructions for Bash.

The simplest way to compile Bash is:

1. `cd` to the directory containing the source code and type '`./configure`' to configure Bash for your system. If you're using `csh` on an old version of System V, you might need to type '`sh ./configure`' instead to prevent `csh` from trying to execute `configure` itself.

   Running `configure` takes some time. While running, it prints messages telling which features it is checking for.

2. Type '`make`' to compile Bash and build the `bashbug` bug reporting script.

3. Optionally, type '`make tests`' to run the Bash test suite.

4. Type '`make install`' to install `bash` and `bashbug`. This will also install the manual pages and Info file.

The `configure` shell script attempts to guess correct values for various system-dependent variables used during compilation. It uses those values to create a `Makefile` in each directory of the package (the top directory, the `builtins`, `doc`, and `support` directories, each directory under `lib`, and several others). It also creates a `config.h` file containing system-dependent definitions. Finally, it creates a shell script named `config.status` that you can run in the future to recreate the current configuration, a file `config.cache` that saves the results of its tests to speed up reconfiguring, and a file `config.log` containing compiler output (useful mainly for debugging `configure`). If at some point `config.cache` contains results you don't want to keep, you may remove or edit it.

To find out more about the options and arguments that the `configure` script understands, type

```
bash-2.04$ ./configure --help
```

at the Bash prompt in your Bash source directory.

If you need to do unusual things to compile Bash, please try to figure out how `configure` could check whether or not to do them, and mail diffs or instructions to `bash-maintainers@gnu.org` so they can be considered for the next release.

The file `configure.ac` is used to create `configure` by a program called Autoconf. You only need `configure.ac` if you want to change it or regenerate `configure` using a newer version of Autoconf. If you do this, make sure you are using Autoconf version 2.50 or newer.

You can remove the program binaries and object files from the source code directory by typing '`make clean`'. To also remove the files that `configure` created (so you can compile Bash for a different kind of computer), type '`make distclean`'.

10.2 Compilers and Options

Some systems require unusual options for compilation or linking that the `configure` script does not know about. You can give `configure` initial values for variables by setting them in the environment. Using a Bourne-compatible shell, you can do that on the command line like this:

        CC=c89 CFLAGS=-O2 LIBS=-lposix ./configure

On systems that have the `env` program, you can do it like this:

        env CPPFLAGS=-I/usr/local/include LDFLAGS=-s ./configure

The configuration process uses GCC to build Bash if it is available.

10.3 Compiling For Multiple Architectures

You can compile Bash for more than one kind of computer at the same time, by placing the object files for each architecture in their own directory. To do this, you must use a version of `make` that supports the `VPATH` variable, such as GNU `make`. `cd` to the directory where you want the object files and executables to go and run the `configure` script from the source directory. You may need to supply the `--srcdir=PATH` argument to tell `configure` where the source files are. `configure` automatically checks for the source code in the directory that `configure` is in and in '..'.

If you have to use a `make` that does not supports the `VPATH` variable, you can compile Bash for one architecture at a time in the source code directory. After you have installed Bash for one architecture, use '`make distclean`' before reconfiguring for another architecture.

Alternatively, if your system supports symbolic links, you can use the `support/mkclone` script to create a build tree which has symbolic links back to each file in the source directory. Here's an example that creates a build directory in the current directory from a source directory /usr/gnu/src/bash-2.0:

        bash /usr/gnu/src/bash-2.0/support/mkclone -s /usr/gnu/src/bash-2.0 .

The `mkclone` script requires Bash, so you must have already built Bash for at least one architecture before you can create build directories for other architectures.

10.4 Installation Names

By default, '`make install`' will install into /usr/local/bin, /usr/local/man, etc. You can specify an installation prefix other than /usr/local by giving `configure` the option `--prefix=PATH`, or by specifying a value for the `DESTDIR` '`make`' variable when running '`make install`'.

You can specify separate installation prefixes for architecture-specific files and architecture-independent files. If you give `configure` the option `--exec-prefix=PATH`, '`make install`' will use *PATH* as the prefix for installing programs and libraries. Documentation and other data files will still use the regular prefix.

10.5 Specifying the System Type

There may be some features `configure` can not figure out automatically, but need to determine by the type of host Bash will run on. Usually `configure` can figure that out, but

if it prints a message saying it can not guess the host type, give it the `--host=TYPE` option.
'TYPE' can either be a short name for the system type, such as 'sun4', or a canonical name
with three fields: 'CPU-COMPANY-SYSTEM' (e.g., 'i386-unknown-freebsd4.2').

See the file `support/config.sub` for the possible values of each field.

10.6 Sharing Defaults

If you want to set default values for `configure` scripts to share, you can create a site
shell script called `config.site` that gives default values for variables like `CC`, `cache_`
`file`, and `prefix`. `configure` looks for `PREFIX/share/config.site` if it exists, then
`PREFIX/etc/config.site` if it exists. Or, you can set the `CONFIG_SITE` environment variable to the location of the site script. A warning: the Bash `configure` looks for a site
script, but not all `configure` scripts do.

10.7 Operation Controls

`configure` recognizes the following options to control how it operates.

`--cache-file=file`
> Use and save the results of the tests in *file* instead of `./config.cache`. Set *file*
> to `/dev/null` to disable caching, for debugging `configure`.

`--help`   Print a summary of the options to `configure`, and exit.

`--quiet`
`--silent`
`-q`   Do not print messages saying which checks are being made.

`--srcdir=dir`
> Look for the Bash source code in directory *dir*. Usually `configure` can deter-
> mine that directory automatically.

`--version`
> Print the version of Autoconf used to generate the `configure` script, and exit.

`configure` also accepts some other, not widely used, boilerplate options. 'configure
--help' prints the complete list.

10.8 Optional Features

The Bash `configure` has a number of `--enable-feature` options, where *feature* indicates
an optional part of Bash. There are also several `--with-package` options, where *package*
is something like 'bash-malloc' or 'purify'. To turn off the default use of a package, use
`--without-package`. To configure Bash without a feature that is enabled by default, use
`--disable-feature`.

Here is a complete list of the `--enable-` and `--with-` options that the Bash `configure`
recognizes.

`--with-afs`
> Define if you are using the Andrew File System from Transarc.

`--with-bash-malloc`

> Use the Bash version of `malloc` in the directory `lib/malloc`. This is not the same `malloc` that appears in GNU libc, but an older version originally derived from the 4.2 BSD `malloc`. This `malloc` is very fast, but wastes some space on each allocation. This option is enabled by default. The `NOTES` file contains a list of systems for which this should be turned off, and `configure` disables this option automatically for a number of systems.

`--with-curses`

> Use the curses library instead of the termcap library. This should be supplied if your system has an inadequate or incomplete termcap database.

`--with-gnu-malloc`

> A synonym for `--with-bash-malloc`.

`--with-installed-readline[=PREFIX]`

> Define this to make Bash link with a locally-installed version of Readline rather than the version in `lib/readline`. This works only with Readline 5.0 and later versions. If *PREFIX* is `yes` or not supplied, `configure` uses the values of the make variables `includedir` and `libdir`, which are subdirectories of `prefix` by default, to find the installed version of Readline if it is not in the standard system include and library directories. If *PREFIX* is `no`, Bash links with the version in `lib/readline`. If *PREFIX* is set to any other value, `configure` treats it as a directory pathname and looks for the installed version of Readline in subdirectories of that directory (include files in *PREFIX*/`include` and the library in *PREFIX*/`lib`).

`--with-purify`

> Define this to use the Purify memory allocation checker from Rational Software.

`--enable-minimal-config`

> This produces a shell with minimal features, close to the historical Bourne shell.

There are several `--enable-` options that alter how Bash is compiled and linked, rather than changing run-time features.

`--enable-largefile`

> Enable support for large files (`http://www.sas.com/standards/large_file/x_open.20Mar96.html`) if the operating system requires special compiler options to build programs which can access large files. This is enabled by default, if the operating system provides large file support.

`--enable-profiling`

> This builds a Bash binary that produces profiling information to be processed by `gprof` each time it is executed.

`--enable-static-link`

> This causes Bash to be linked statically, if `gcc` is being used. This could be used to build a version to use as root's shell.

The '`minimal-config`' option can be used to disable all of the following options, but it is processed first, so individual options may be enabled using '`enable-feature`'.

All of the following options except for 'disabled-builtins', 'direxpand-default', and 'xpg-echo-default' are enabled by default, unless the operating system does not provide the necessary support.

`--enable-alias`

> Allow alias expansion and include the `alias` and `unalias` builtins (see Section 6.6 [Aliases], page 90).

`--enable-arith-for-command`

> Include support for the alternate form of the `for` command that behaves like the C language `for` statement (see Section 3.2.4.1 [Looping Constructs], page 10).

`--enable-array-variables`

> Include support for one-dimensional array shell variables (see Section 6.7 [Arrays], page 91).

`--enable-bang-history`

> Include support for `csh`-like history substitution (see Section 9.3 [History Interaction], page 139).

`--enable-brace-expansion`

> Include `csh`-like brace expansion (`b{a,b}c` $\mapsto$ `bac bbc`). See Section 3.5.1 [Brace Expansion], page 21, for a complete description.

`--enable-casemod-attributes`

> Include support for case-modifying attributes in the `declare` builtin and assignment statements. Variables with the *uppercase* attribute, for example, will have their values converted to uppercase upon assignment.

`--enable-casemod-expansion`

> Include support for case-modifying word expansions.

`--enable-command-timing`

> Include support for recognizing `time` as a reserved word and for displaying timing statistics for the pipeline following `time` (see Section 3.2.2 [Pipelines], page 8). This allows pipelines as well as shell builtins and functions to be timed.

`--enable-cond-command`

> Include support for the `[[` conditional command. (see Section 3.2.4.2 [Conditional Constructs], page 10).

`--enable-cond-regexp`

> Include support for matching POSIX regular expressions using the '=~' binary operator in the `[[` conditional command. (see Section 3.2.4.2 [Conditional Constructs], page 10).

`--enable-coprocesses`

> Include support for coprocesses and the `coproc` reserved word (see Section 3.2.2 [Pipelines], page 8).

`--enable-debugger`

> Include support for the bash debugger (distributed separately).

`--enable-direxpand-default`

> Cause the `direxpand` shell option (see Section 4.3.2 [The Shopt Builtin], page 64) to be enabled by default when the shell starts. It is normally disabled by default.

`--enable-directory-stack`

> Include support for a `csh`-like directory stack and the `pushd`, `popd`, and `dirs` builtins (see Section 6.8 [The Directory Stack], page 93).

`--enable-disabled-builtins`

> Allow builtin commands to be invoked via 'builtin xxx' even after xxx has been disabled using 'enable -n xxx'. See Section 4.2 [Bash Builtins], page 49, for details of the `builtin` and `enable` builtin commands.

`--enable-dparen-arithmetic`

> Include support for the `((...))` command (see Section 3.2.4.2 [Conditional Constructs], page 10).

`--enable-extended-glob`

> Include support for the extended pattern matching features described above under Section 3.5.8.1 [Pattern Matching], page 31.

`--enable-extended-glob-default`

> Set the default value of the *extglob* shell option described above under Section 4.3.2 [The Shopt Builtin], page 64, to be enabled.

`--enable-function-import`

> Include support for importing function definitions exported by another instance of the shell from the environment. This option is enabled by default.

`--enable-glob-asciirange-default`

> Set the default value of the *globasciiranges* shell option described above under Section 4.3.2 [The Shopt Builtin], page 64, to be enabled. This controls the behavior of character ranges when used in pattern matching bracket expressions.

`--enable-help-builtin`

> Include the `help` builtin, which displays help on shell builtins and variables (see Section 4.2 [Bash Builtins], page 49).

`--enable-history`

> Include command history and the `fc` and `history` builtin commands (see Section 9.1 [Bash History Facilities], page 137).

`--enable-job-control`

> This enables the job control features (see Chapter 7 [Job Control], page 100), if the operating system supports them.

`--enable-multibyte`

> This enables support for multibyte characters if the operating system provides the necessary support.

`--enable-net-redirections`

> This enables the special handling of filenames of the form `/dev/tcp/host/port` and `/dev/udp/host/port` when used in redirections (see Section 3.6 [Redirections], page 32).

`--enable-process-substitution`

> This enables process substitution (see Section 3.5.6 [Process Substitution], page 30) if the operating system provides the necessary support.

`--enable-progcomp`

> Enable the programmable completion facilities (see Section 8.6 [Programmable Completion], page 129). If Readline is not enabled, this option has no effect.

`--enable-prompt-string-decoding`

> Turn on the interpretation of a number of backslash-escaped characters in the $PS1, $PS2, $PS3, and $PS4 prompt strings. See Section 6.9 [Controlling the Prompt], page 94, for a complete list of prompt string escape sequences.

`--enable-readline`

> Include support for command-line editing and history with the Bash version of the Readline library (see Chapter 8 [Command Line Editing], page 104).

`--enable-restricted`

> Include support for a *restricted shell*. If this is enabled, Bash, when called as `rbash`, enters a restricted mode. See Section 6.10 [The Restricted Shell], page 95, for a description of restricted mode.

`--enable-select`

> Include the `select` compound command, which allows the generation of simple menus (see Section 3.2.4.2 [Conditional Constructs], page 10).

`--enable-separate-helpfiles`

> Use external files for the documentation displayed by the `help` builtin instead of storing the text internally.

`--enable-single-help-strings`

> Store the text displayed by the `help` builtin as a single string for each help topic. This aids in translating the text to different languages. You may need to disable this if your compiler cannot handle very long string literals.

`--enable-strict-posix-default`

> Make Bash POSIX-conformant by default (see Section 6.11 [Bash POSIX Mode], page 96).

`--enable-usg-echo-default`

> A synonym for `--enable-xpg-echo-default`.

`--enable-xpg-echo-default`

> Make the `echo` builtin expand backslash-escaped characters by default, without requiring the `-e` option. This sets the default value of the `xpg_echo` shell option to `on`, which makes the Bash `echo` behave more like the version specified in the Single Unix Specification, version 3. See Section 4.2 [Bash Builtins], page 49, for a description of the escape sequences that `echo` recognizes.

The file `config-top.h` contains C Preprocessor '#define' statements for options which are not settable from `configure`. Some of these are not meant to be changed; beware of the consequences if you do. Read the comments associated with each definition for more information about its effect.

Appendix A Reporting Bugs

Please report all bugs you find in Bash. But first, you should make sure that it really is a bug, and that it appears in the latest version of Bash. The latest version of Bash is always available for FTP from `ftp://ftp.gnu.org/pub/gnu/bash/`.

Once you have determined that a bug actually exists, use the `bashbug` command to submit a bug report. If you have a fix, you are encouraged to mail that as well! Suggestions and 'philosophical' bug reports may be mailed to `bug-bash@gnu.org` or posted to the Usenet newsgroup `gnu.bash.bug`.

All bug reports should include:

- The version number of Bash.
- The hardware and operating system.
- The compiler used to compile Bash.
- A description of the bug behaviour.
- A short script or 'recipe' which exercises the bug and may be used to reproduce it.

`bashbug` inserts the first three items automatically into the template it provides for filing a bug report.

Please send all reports concerning this manual to `bug-bash@gnu.org`.

Appendix B Major Differences From The Bourne Shell

Bash implements essentially the same grammar, parameter and variable expansion, redirection, and quoting as the Bourne Shell. Bash uses the POSIX standard as the specification of how these features are to be implemented. There are some differences between the traditional Bourne shell and Bash; this section quickly details the differences of significance. A number of these differences are explained in greater depth in previous sections. This section uses the version of **sh** included in SVR4.2 (the last version of the historical Bourne shell) as the baseline reference.

- Bash is POSIX-conformant, even where the POSIX specification differs from traditional **sh** behavior (see Section 6.11 [Bash POSIX Mode], page 96).

- Bash has multi-character invocation options (see Section 6.1 [Invoking Bash], page 82).

- Bash has command-line editing (see Chapter 8 [Command Line Editing], page 104) and the **bind** builtin.

- Bash provides a programmable word completion mechanism (see Section 8.6 [Programmable Completion], page 129), and builtin commands **complete**, **compgen**, and **compopt**, to manipulate it.

- Bash has command history (see Section 9.1 [Bash History Facilities], page 137) and the **history** and **fc** builtins to manipulate it. The Bash history list maintains timestamp information and uses the value of the **HISTTIMEFORMAT** variable to display it.

- Bash implements **csh**-like history expansion (see Section 9.3 [History Interaction], page 139).

- Bash has one-dimensional array variables (see Section 6.7 [Arrays], page 91), and the appropriate variable expansions and assignment syntax to use them. Several of the Bash builtins take options to act on arrays. Bash provides a number of built-in array variables.

- The $'...' quoting syntax, which expands ANSI-C backslash-escaped characters in the text between the single quotes, is supported (see Section 3.1.2.4 [ANSI-C Quoting], page 6).

- Bash supports the $"..." quoting syntax to do locale-specific translation of the characters between the double quotes. The -D, --dump-strings, and --dump-po-strings invocation options list the translatable strings found in a script (see Section 3.1.2.5 [Locale Translation], page 7).

- Bash implements the ! keyword to negate the return value of a pipeline (see Section 3.2.2 [Pipelines], page 8). Very useful when an **if** statement needs to act only if a test fails. The Bash '-o pipefail' option to **set** will cause a pipeline to return a failure status if any command fails.

- Bash has the **time** reserved word and command timing (see Section 3.2.2 [Pipelines], page 8). The display of the timing statistics may be controlled with the **TIMEFORMAT** variable.

- Bash implements the **for ((expr1 ; expr2 ; expr3))** arithmetic for command, similar to the C language (see Section 3.2.4.1 [Looping Constructs], page 10).

- Bash includes the **select** compound command, which allows the generation of simple menus (see Section 3.2.4.2 [Conditional Constructs], page 10).

- Bash includes the `[[` compound command, which makes conditional testing part of the shell grammar (see Section 3.2.4.2 [Conditional Constructs], page 10), including optional regular expression matching.

- Bash provides optional case-insensitive matching for the **case** and `[[` constructs.

- Bash includes brace expansion (see Section 3.5.1 [Brace Expansion], page 21) and tilde expansion (see Section 3.5.2 [Tilde Expansion], page 22).

- Bash implements command aliases and the **alias** and **unalias** builtins (see Section 6.6 [Aliases], page 90).

- Bash provides shell arithmetic, the `((` compound command (see Section 3.2.4.2 [Conditional Constructs], page 10), and arithmetic expansion (see Section 6.5 [Shell Arithmetic], page 89).

- Variables present in the shell's initial environment are automatically exported to child processes. The Bourne shell does not normally do this unless the variables are explicitly marked using the **export** command.

- Bash supports the '+=' assignment operator, which appends to the value of the variable named on the left hand side.

- Bash includes the POSIX pattern removal '%', '#', '%%' and '##' expansions to remove leading or trailing substrings from variable values (see Section 3.5.3 [Shell Parameter Expansion], page 23).

- The expansion `${#xx}`, which returns the length of `${xx}`, is supported (see Section 3.5.3 [Shell Parameter Expansion], page 23).

- The expansion `${var:`*offset*`[:`*length*`]}`, which expands to the substring of **var**'s value of length *length*, beginning at *offset*, is present (see Section 3.5.3 [Shell Parameter Expansion], page 23).

- The expansion `${var/[/]`*pattern*`[/`*replacement*`]}`, which matches *pattern* and replaces it with *replacement* in the value of **var**, is available (see Section 3.5.3 [Shell Parameter Expansion], page 23).

- The expansion `${!`*prefix*`*}` expansion, which expands to the names of all shell variables whose names begin with *prefix*, is available (see Section 3.5.3 [Shell Parameter Expansion], page 23).

- Bash has *indirect* variable expansion using `${!word}` (see Section 3.5.3 [Shell Parameter Expansion], page 23).

- Bash can expand positional parameters beyond $9 using `${`*num*`}`.

- The POSIX `$()` form of command substitution is implemented (see Section 3.5.4 [Command Substitution], page 29), and preferred to the Bourne shell's `` ` ` `` (which is also implemented for backwards compatibility).

- Bash has process substitution (see Section 3.5.6 [Process Substitution], page 30).

- Bash automatically assigns variables that provide information about the current user (**UID**, **EUID**, and **GROUPS**), the current host (**HOSTTYPE**, **OSTYPE**, **MACHTYPE**, and **HOSTNAME**), and the instance of Bash that is running (**BASH**, **BASH_VERSION**, and **BASH_VERSINFO**). See Section 5.2 [Bash Variables], page 71, for details.

- The **IFS** variable is used to split only the results of expansion, not all words (see Section 3.5.7 [Word Splitting], page 30). This closes a longstanding shell security hole.

- The filename expansion bracket expression code uses '!' and '^' to negate the set of characters between the brackets. The Bourne shell uses only '!'.

- Bash implements the full set of POSIX filename expansion operators, including *character classes*, *equivalence classes*, and *collating symbols* (see Section 3.5.8 [Filename Expansion], page 30).

- Bash implements extended pattern matching features when the `extglob` shell option is enabled (see Section 3.5.8.1 [Pattern Matching], page 31).

- It is possible to have a variable and a function with the same name; `sh` does not separate the two name spaces.

- Bash functions are permitted to have local variables using the `local` builtin, and thus useful recursive functions may be written (see Section 4.2 [Bash Builtins], page 49).

- Variable assignments preceding commands affect only that command, even builtins and functions (see Section 3.7.4 [Environment], page 38). In `sh`, all variable assignments preceding commands are global unless the command is executed from the file system.

- Bash performs filename expansion on filenames specified as operands to input and output redirection operators (see Section 3.6 [Redirections], page 32).

- Bash contains the '<>' redirection operator, allowing a file to be opened for both reading and writing, and the '&>' redirection operator, for directing standard output and standard error to the same file (see Section 3.6 [Redirections], page 32).

- Bash includes the '<<<' redirection operator, allowing a string to be used as the standard input to a command.

- Bash implements the '[n]<&word' and '[n]>&word' redirection operators, which move one file descriptor to another.

- Bash treats a number of filenames specially when they are used in redirection operators (see Section 3.6 [Redirections], page 32).

- Bash can open network connections to arbitrary machines and services with the redirection operators (see Section 3.6 [Redirections], page 32).

- The `noclobber` option is available to avoid overwriting existing files with output redirection (see Section 4.3.1 [The Set Builtin], page 60). The '>|' redirection operator may be used to override `noclobber`.

- The Bash `cd` and `pwd` builtins (see Section 4.1 [Bourne Shell Builtins], page 42) each take -L and -P options to switch between logical and physical modes.

- Bash allows a function to override a builtin with the same name, and provides access to that builtin's functionality within the function via the `builtin` and `command` builtins (see Section 4.2 [Bash Builtins], page 49).

- The `command` builtin allows selective disabling of functions when command lookup is performed (see Section 4.2 [Bash Builtins], page 49).

- Individual builtins may be enabled or disabled using the `enable` builtin (see Section 4.2 [Bash Builtins], page 49).

- The Bash `exec` builtin takes additional options that allow users to control the contents of the environment passed to the executed command, and what the zeroth argument to the command is to be (see Section 4.1 [Bourne Shell Builtins], page 42).

- Shell functions may be exported to children via the environment using `export -f` (see Section 3.3 [Shell Functions], page 17).

- The Bash `export`, `readonly`, and `declare` builtins can take a `-f` option to act on shell functions, a `-p` option to display variables with various attributes set in a format that can be used as shell input, a `-n` option to remove various variable attributes, and 'name=value' arguments to set variable attributes and values simultaneously.

- The Bash `hash` builtin allows a name to be associated with an arbitrary filename, even when that filename cannot be found by searching the `$PATH`, using 'hash -p' (see Section 4.1 [Bourne Shell Builtins], page 42).

- Bash includes a `help` builtin for quick reference to shell facilities (see Section 4.2 [Bash Builtins], page 49).

- The `printf` builtin is available to display formatted output (see Section 4.2 [Bash Builtins], page 49).

- The Bash `read` builtin (see Section 4.2 [Bash Builtins], page 49) will read a line ending in '\' with the `-r` option, and will use the `REPLY` variable as a default if no non-option arguments are supplied. The Bash `read` builtin also accepts a prompt string with the `-p` option and will use Readline to obtain the line when given the `-e` option. The `read` builtin also has additional options to control input: the `-s` option will turn off echoing of input characters as they are read, the `-t` option will allow `read` to time out if input does not arrive within a specified number of seconds, the `-n` option will allow reading only a specified number of characters rather than a full line, and the `-d` option will read until a particular character rather than newline.

- The `return` builtin may be used to abort execution of scripts executed with the . or `source` builtins (see Section 4.1 [Bourne Shell Builtins], page 42).

- Bash includes the `shopt` builtin, for finer control of shell optional capabilities (see Section 4.3.2 [The Shopt Builtin], page 64), and allows these options to be set and unset at shell invocation (see Section 6.1 [Invoking Bash], page 82).

- Bash has much more optional behavior controllable with the `set` builtin (see Section 4.3.1 [The Set Builtin], page 60).

- The '-x' (`xtrace`) option displays commands other than simple commands when performing an execution trace (see Section 4.3.1 [The Set Builtin], page 60).

- The `test` builtin (see Section 4.1 [Bourne Shell Builtins], page 42) is slightly different, as it implements the POSIX algorithm, which specifies the behavior based on the number of arguments.

- Bash includes the `caller` builtin, which displays the context of any active subroutine call (a shell function or a script executed with the . or `source` builtins). This supports the bash debugger.

- The `trap` builtin (see Section 4.1 [Bourne Shell Builtins], page 42) allows a DEBUG pseudo-signal specification, similar to EXIT. Commands specified with a DEBUG trap are executed before every simple command, `for` command, `case` command, `select` command, every arithmetic `for` command, and before the first command executes in a shell function. The DEBUG trap is not inherited by shell functions unless the function has been given the `trace` attribute or the `functrace` option has been enabled using the `shopt` builtin. The `extdebug` shell option has additional effects on the DEBUG trap.

  The `trap` builtin (see Section 4.1 [Bourne Shell Builtins], page 42) allows an ERR pseudo-signal specification, similar to EXIT and DEBUG. Commands specified with an ERR trap are executed after a simple command fails, with a few exceptions. The ERR trap is not inherited by shell functions unless the -o errtrace option to the set builtin is enabled.

The trap builtin (see Section 4.1 [Bourne Shell Builtins], page 42) allows a RETURN pseudo-signal specification, similar to EXIT and DEBUG. Commands specified with an RETURN trap are executed before execution resumes after a shell function or a shell script executed with . or source returns. The RETURN trap is not inherited by shell functions unless the function has been given the trace attribute or the functrace option has been enabled using the shopt builtin.

- The Bash type builtin is more extensive and gives more information about the names it finds (see Section 4.2 [Bash Builtins], page 49).

- The Bash umask builtin permits a -p option to cause the output to be displayed in the form of a umask command that may be reused as input (see Section 4.1 [Bourne Shell Builtins], page 42).

- Bash implements a csh-like directory stack, and provides the pushd, popd, and dirs builtins to manipulate it (see Section 6.8 [The Directory Stack], page 93). Bash also makes the directory stack visible as the value of the DIRSTACK shell variable.

- Bash interprets special backslash-escaped characters in the prompt strings when interactive (see Section 6.9 [Controlling the Prompt], page 94).

- The Bash restricted mode is more useful (see Section 6.10 [The Restricted Shell], page 95); the SVR4.2 shell restricted mode is too limited.

- The disown builtin can remove a job from the internal shell job table (see Section 7.2 [Job Control Builtins], page 101) or suppress the sending of SIGHUP to a job when the shell exits as the result of a SIGHUP.

- Bash includes a number of features to support a separate debugger for shell scripts.

- The SVR4.2 shell has two privilege-related builtins (mldmode and priv) not present in Bash.

- Bash does not have the stop or newgrp builtins.

- Bash does not use the SHACCT variable or perform shell accounting.

- The SVR4.2 sh uses a TIMEOUT variable like Bash uses TMOUT.

More features unique to Bash may be found in Chapter 6 [Bash Features], page 82.

B.1 Implementation Differences From The SVR4.2 Shell

Since Bash is a completely new implementation, it does not suffer from many of the limitations of the SVR4.2 shell. For instance:

- Bash does not fork a subshell when redirecting into or out of a shell control structure such as an if or while statement.

- Bash does not allow unbalanced quotes. The SVR4.2 shell will silently insert a needed closing quote at EOF under certain circumstances. This can be the cause of some hard-to-find errors.

- The SVR4.2 shell uses a baroque memory management scheme based on trapping SIGSEGV. If the shell is started from a process with SIGSEGV blocked (e.g., by using the system() C library function call), it misbehaves badly.

- In a questionable attempt at security, the SVR4.2 shell, when invoked without the `-p` option, will alter its real and effective UID and GID if they are less than some magic threshold value, commonly 100. This can lead to unexpected results.

- The SVR4.2 shell does not allow users to trap `SIGSEGV`, `SIGALRM`, or `SIGCHLD`.

- The SVR4.2 shell does not allow the `IFS`, `MAILCHECK`, `PATH`, `PS1`, or `PS2` variables to be unset.

- The SVR4.2 shell treats '^' as the undocumented equivalent of '|'.

- Bash allows multiple option arguments when it is invoked (`-x -v`); the SVR4.2 shell allows only one option argument (`-xv`). In fact, some versions of the shell dump core if the second argument begins with a '-'.

- The SVR4.2 shell exits a script if any builtin fails; Bash exits a script only if one of the POSIX special builtins fails, and only for certain failures, as enumerated in the POSIX standard.

- The SVR4.2 shell behaves differently when invoked as `jsh` (it turns on job control).

Appendix C GNU Free Documentation License

Version 1.3, 3 November 2008

Copyright © 2000, 2001, 2002, 2007, 2008 Free Software Foundation, Inc.
http://fsf.org/

0. PREAMBLE

The purpose of this License is to make a manual, textbook, or other functional and useful document *free* in the sense of freedom: to assure everyone the effective freedom to copy and redistribute it, with or without modifying it, either commercially or non-commercially. Secondarily, this License preserves for the author and publisher a way to get credit for their work, while not being considered responsible for modifications made by others.

This License is a kind of "copyleft", which means that derivative works of the document must themselves be free in the same sense. It complements the GNU General Public License, which is a copyleft license designed for free software.

We have designed this License in order to use it for manuals for free software, because free software needs free documentation: a free program should come with manuals providing the same freedoms that the software does. But this License is not limited to software manuals; it can be used for any textual work, regardless of subject matter or whether it is published as a printed book. We recommend this License principally for works whose purpose is instruction or reference.

1. APPLICABILITY AND DEFINITIONS

This License applies to any manual or other work, in any medium, that contains a notice placed by the copyright holder saying it can be distributed under the terms of this License. Such a notice grants a world-wide, royalty-free license, unlimited in duration, to use that work under the conditions stated herein. The "Document", below, refers to any such manual or work. Any member of the public is a licensee, and is addressed as "you". You accept the license if you copy, modify or distribute the work in a way requiring permission under copyright law.

A "Modified Version" of the Document means any work containing the Document or a portion of it, either copied verbatim, or with modifications and/or translated into another language.

A "Secondary Section" is a named appendix or a front-matter section of the Document that deals exclusively with the relationship of the publishers or authors of the Document to the Document's overall subject (or to related matters) and contains nothing that could fall directly within that overall subject. (Thus, if the Document is in part a textbook of mathematics, a Secondary Section may not explain any mathematics.) The relationship could be a matter of historical connection with the subject or with related matters, or of legal, commercial, philosophical, ethical or political position regarding them.

The "Invariant Sections" are certain Secondary Sections whose titles are designated, as being those of Invariant Sections, in the notice that says that the Document is released under this License. If a section does not fit the above definition of Secondary then it is not allowed to be designated as Invariant. The Document may contain zero Invariant Sections. If the Document does not identify any Invariant Sections then there are none.

The "Cover Texts" are certain short passages of text that are listed, as Front-Cover Texts or Back-Cover Texts, in the notice that says that the Document is released under this License. A Front-Cover Text may be at most 5 words, and a Back-Cover Text may be at most 25 words.

A "Transparent" copy of the Document means a machine-readable copy, represented in a format whose specification is available to the general public, that is suitable for revising the document straightforwardly with generic text editors or (for images composed of pixels) generic paint programs or (for drawings) some widely available drawing editor, and that is suitable for input to text formatters or for automatic translation to a variety of formats suitable for input to text formatters. A copy made in an otherwise Transparent file format whose markup, or absence of markup, has been arranged to thwart or discourage subsequent modification by readers is not Transparent. An image format is not Transparent if used for any substantial amount of text. A copy that is not "Transparent" is called "Opaque".

Examples of suitable formats for Transparent copies include plain ASCII without markup, Texinfo input format, LaTeX input format, SGML or XML using a publicly available DTD, and standard-conforming simple HTML, PostScript or PDF designed for human modification. Examples of transparent image formats include PNG, XCF and JPG. Opaque formats include proprietary formats that can be read and edited only by proprietary word processors, SGML or XML for which the DTD and/or processing tools are not generally available, and the machine-generated HTML, PostScript or PDF produced by some word processors for output purposes only.

The "Title Page" means, for a printed book, the title page itself, plus such following pages as are needed to hold, legibly, the material this License requires to appear in the title page. For works in formats which do not have any title page as such, "Title Page" means the text near the most prominent appearance of the work's title, preceding the beginning of the body of the text.

The "publisher" means any person or entity that distributes copies of the Document to the public.

A section "Entitled XYZ" means a named subunit of the Document whose title either is precisely XYZ or contains XYZ in parentheses following text that translates XYZ in another language. (Here XYZ stands for a specific section name mentioned below, such as "Acknowledgements", "Dedications", "Endorsements", or "History".) To "Preserve the Title" of such a section when you modify the Document means that it remains a section "Entitled XYZ" according to this definition.

The Document may include Warranty Disclaimers next to the notice which states that this License applies to the Document. These Warranty Disclaimers are considered to be included by reference in this License, but only as regards disclaiming warranties: any other implication that these Warranty Disclaimers may have is void and has no effect on the meaning of this License.

2. VERBATIM COPYING

You may copy and distribute the Document in any medium, either commercially or noncommercially, provided that this License, the copyright notices, and the license notice saying this License applies to the Document are reproduced in all copies, and that you add no other conditions whatsoever to those of this License. You may not use technical measures to obstruct or control the reading or further copying of the copies you make or distribute. However, you may accept compensation in exchange for copies. If you distribute a large enough number of copies you must also follow the conditions in section 3.

You may also lend copies, under the same conditions stated above, and you may publicly display copies.

3. COPYING IN QUANTITY

If you publish printed copies (or copies in media that commonly have printed covers) of the Document, numbering more than 100, and the Document's license notice requires Cover Texts, you must enclose the copies in covers that carry, clearly and legibly, all these Cover Texts: Front-Cover Texts on the front cover, and Back-Cover Texts on the back cover. Both covers must also clearly and legibly identify you as the publisher of these copies. The front cover must present the full title with all words of the title equally prominent and visible. You may add other material on the covers in addition. Copying with changes limited to the covers, as long as they preserve the title of the Document and satisfy these conditions, can be treated as verbatim copying in other respects.

If the required texts for either cover are too voluminous to fit legibly, you should put the first ones listed (as many as fit reasonably) on the actual cover, and continue the rest onto adjacent pages.

If you publish or distribute Opaque copies of the Document numbering more than 100, you must either include a machine-readable Transparent copy along with each Opaque copy, or state in or with each Opaque copy a computer-network location from which the general network-using public has access to download using public-standard network protocols a complete Transparent copy of the Document, free of added material. If you use the latter option, you must take reasonably prudent steps, when you begin distribution of Opaque copies in quantity, to ensure that this Transparent copy will remain thus accessible at the stated location until at least one year after the last time you distribute an Opaque copy (directly or through your agents or retailers) of that edition to the public.

It is requested, but not required, that you contact the authors of the Document well before redistributing any large number of copies, to give them a chance to provide you with an updated version of the Document.

4. MODIFICATIONS

You may copy and distribute a Modified Version of the Document under the conditions of sections 2 and 3 above, provided that you release the Modified Version under precisely this License, with the Modified Version filling the role of the Document, thus licensing distribution and modification of the Modified Version to whoever possesses a copy of it. In addition, you must do these things in the Modified Version:

A. Use in the Title Page (and on the covers, if any) a title distinct from that of the Document, and from those of previous versions (which should, if there were any, be listed in the History section of the Document). You may use the same title as a previous version if the original publisher of that version gives permission.

B. List on the Title Page, as authors, one or more persons or entities responsible for authorship of the modifications in the Modified Version, together with at least five of the principal authors of the Document (all of its principal authors, if it has fewer than five), unless they release you from this requirement.

C. State on the Title page the name of the publisher of the Modified Version, as the publisher.

D. Preserve all the copyright notices of the Document.

E. Add an appropriate copyright notice for your modifications adjacent to the other copyright notices.

F. Include, immediately after the copyright notices, a license notice giving the public permission to use the Modified Version under the terms of this License, in the form shown in the Addendum below.

G. Preserve in that license notice the full lists of Invariant Sections and required Cover Texts given in the Document's license notice.

H. Include an unaltered copy of this License.

I. Preserve the section Entitled "History", Preserve its Title, and add to it an item stating at least the title, year, new authors, and publisher of the Modified Version as given on the Title Page. If there is no section Entitled "History" in the Document, create one stating the title, year, authors, and publisher of the Document as given on its Title Page, then add an item describing the Modified Version as stated in the previous sentence.

J. Preserve the network location, if any, given in the Document for public access to a Transparent copy of the Document, and likewise the network locations given in the Document for previous versions it was based on. These may be placed in the "History" section. You may omit a network location for a work that was published at least four years before the Document itself, or if the original publisher of the version it refers to gives permission.

K. For any section Entitled "Acknowledgements" or "Dedications", Preserve the Title of the section, and preserve in the section all the substance and tone of each of the contributor acknowledgements and/or dedications given therein.

L. Preserve all the Invariant Sections of the Document, unaltered in their text and in their titles. Section numbers or the equivalent are not considered part of the section titles.

M. Delete any section Entitled "Endorsements". Such a section may not be included in the Modified Version.

N. Do not retitle any existing section to be Entitled "Endorsements" or to conflict in title with any Invariant Section.

O. Preserve any Warranty Disclaimers.

If the Modified Version includes new front-matter sections or appendices that qualify as Secondary Sections and contain no material copied from the Document, you may at your option designate some or all of these sections as invariant. To do this, add their titles to the list of Invariant Sections in the Modified Version's license notice. These titles must be distinct from any other section titles.

You may add a section Entitled "Endorsements", provided it contains nothing but endorsements of your Modified Version by various parties—for example, statements of peer review or that the text has been approved by an organization as the authoritative definition of a standard.

You may add a passage of up to five words as a Front-Cover Text, and a passage of up to 25 words as a Back-Cover Text, to the end of the list of Cover Texts in the Modified Version. Only one passage of Front-Cover Text and one of Back-Cover Text may be added by (or through arrangements made by) any one entity. If the Document already includes a cover text for the same cover, previously added by you or by arrangement made by the same entity you are acting on behalf of, you may not add another; but you may replace the old one, on explicit permission from the previous publisher that added the old one.

The author(s) and publisher(s) of the Document do not by this License give permission to use their names for publicity for or to assert or imply endorsement of any Modified Version.

5. COMBINING DOCUMENTS

You may combine the Document with other documents released under this License, under the terms defined in section 4 above for modified versions, provided that you include in the combination all of the Invariant Sections of all of the original documents, unmodified, and list them all as Invariant Sections of your combined work in its license notice, and that you preserve all their Warranty Disclaimers.

The combined work need only contain one copy of this License, and multiple identical Invariant Sections may be replaced with a single copy. If there are multiple Invariant Sections with the same name but different contents, make the title of each such section unique by adding at the end of it, in parentheses, the name of the original author or publisher of that section if known, or else a unique number. Make the same adjustment to the section titles in the list of Invariant Sections in the license notice of the combined work.

In the combination, you must combine any sections Entitled "History" in the various original documents, forming one section Entitled "History"; likewise combine any sections Entitled "Acknowledgements", and any sections Entitled "Dedications". You must delete all sections Entitled "Endorsements."

6. COLLECTIONS OF DOCUMENTS

You may make a collection consisting of the Document and other documents released under this License, and replace the individual copies of this License in the various documents with a single copy that is included in the collection, provided that you follow the rules of this License for verbatim copying of each of the documents in all other respects.

You may extract a single document from such a collection, and distribute it individually under this License, provided you insert a copy of this License into the extracted document, and follow this License in all other respects regarding verbatim copying of that document.

7. AGGREGATION WITH INDEPENDENT WORKS

A compilation of the Document or its derivatives with other separate and independent documents or works, in or on a volume of a storage or distribution medium, is called an "aggregate" if the copyright resulting from the compilation is not used to limit the legal rights of the compilation's users beyond what the individual works permit. When the Document is included in an aggregate, this License does not apply to the other works in the aggregate which are not themselves derivative works of the Document.

If the Cover Text requirement of section 3 is applicable to these copies of the Document, then if the Document is less than one half of the entire aggregate, the Document's Cover Texts may be placed on covers that bracket the Document within the aggregate, or the electronic equivalent of covers if the Document is in electronic form. Otherwise they must appear on printed covers that bracket the whole aggregate.

8. TRANSLATION

Translation is considered a kind of modification, so you may distribute translations of the Document under the terms of section 4. Replacing Invariant Sections with translations requires special permission from their copyright holders, but you may include translations of some or all Invariant Sections in addition to the original versions of these Invariant Sections. You may include a translation of this License, and all the license notices in the Document, and any Warranty Disclaimers, provided that you also include the original English version of this License and the original versions of those notices and disclaimers. In case of a disagreement between the translation and the original version of this License or a notice or disclaimer, the original version will prevail.

If a section in the Document is Entitled "Acknowledgements", "Dedications", or "History", the requirement (section 4) to Preserve its Title (section 1) will typically require changing the actual title.

9. TERMINATION

You may not copy, modify, sublicense, or distribute the Document except as expressly provided under this License. Any attempt otherwise to copy, modify, sublicense, or distribute it is void, and will automatically terminate your rights under this License.

However, if you cease all violation of this License, then your license from a particular copyright holder is reinstated (a) provisionally, unless and until the copyright holder explicitly and finally terminates your license, and (b) permanently, if the copyright holder fails to notify you of the violation by some reasonable means prior to 60 days after the cessation.

Moreover, your license from a particular copyright holder is reinstated permanently if the copyright holder notifies you of the violation by some reasonable means, this is the first time you have received notice of violation of this License (for any work) from that copyright holder, and you cure the violation prior to 30 days after your receipt of the notice.

Termination of your rights under this section does not terminate the licenses of parties who have received copies or rights from you under this License. If your rights have been terminated and not permanently reinstated, receipt of a copy of some or all of the same material does not give you any rights to use it.

10. FUTURE REVISIONS OF THIS LICENSE

The Free Software Foundation may publish new, revised versions of the GNU Free Documentation License from time to time. Such new versions will be similar in spirit to the present version, but may differ in detail to address new problems or concerns. See `http://www.gnu.org/copyleft/`.

Each version of the License is given a distinguishing version number. If the Document specifies that a particular numbered version of this License "or any later version" applies to it, you have the option of following the terms and conditions either of that specified version or of any later version that has been published (not as a draft) by the Free Software Foundation. If the Document does not specify a version number of this License, you may choose any version ever published (not as a draft) by the Free Software Foundation. If the Document specifies that a proxy can decide which future versions of this License can be used, that proxy's public statement of acceptance of a version permanently authorizes you to choose that version for the Document.

11. RELICENSING

"Massive Multiauthor Collaboration Site" (or "MMC Site") means any World Wide Web server that publishes copyrightable works and also provides prominent facilities for anybody to edit those works. A public wiki that anybody can edit is an example of such a server. A "Massive Multiauthor Collaboration" (or "MMC") contained in the site means any set of copyrightable works thus published on the MMC site.

"CC-BY-SA" means the Creative Commons Attribution-Share Alike 3.0 license published by Creative Commons Corporation, a not-for-profit corporation with a principal place of business in San Francisco, California, as well as future copyleft versions of that license published by that same organization.

"Incorporate" means to publish or republish a Document, in whole or in part, as part of another Document.

An MMC is "eligible for relicensing" if it is licensed under this License, and if all works that were first published under this License somewhere other than this MMC, and subsequently incorporated in whole or in part into the MMC, (1) had no cover texts or invariant sections, and (2) were thus incorporated prior to November 1, 2008.

The operator of an MMC Site may republish an MMC contained in the site under CC-BY-SA on the same site at any time before August 1, 2009, provided the MMC is eligible for relicensing.

ADDENDUM: How to use this License for your documents

To use this License in a document you have written, include a copy of the License in the document and put the following copyright and license notices just after the title page:

```
Copyright (C)  year  your name.
Permission is granted to copy, distribute and/or modify this document
under the terms of the GNU Free Documentation License, Version 1.3
or any later version published by the Free Software Foundation;
with no Invariant Sections, no Front-Cover Texts, and no Back-Cover
Texts.  A copy of the license is included in the section entitled ''GNU
Free Documentation License''.
```

If you have Invariant Sections, Front-Cover Texts and Back-Cover Texts, replace the "with. . . Texts." line with this:

```
with the Invariant Sections being list their titles, with
the Front-Cover Texts being list, and with the Back-Cover Texts
being list.
```

If you have Invariant Sections without Cover Texts, or some other combination of the three, merge those two alternatives to suit the situation.

If your document contains nontrivial examples of program code, we recommend releasing these examples in parallel under your choice of free software license, such as the GNU General Public License, to permit their use in free software.

Appendix D Indexes

D.1 Index of Shell Builtin Commands

T

U

W

D.2 Index of Shell Reserved Words

!

[

]

{

}

C

D

E

F

I

S

T

U

W

D.3 Parameter and Variable Index

D.4 Function Index

D.5 Concept Index

CPSIA information can be obtained
at www.ICGtesting.com
Printed in the USA
BVHW091147040720
582960BV00005B/565